A Gift to Posterity on the Laws of Evqaf

Omer Hilmi Effendi, Charles
Robert Tyser, Ahmed Raik Effendi

The Making of Modern Law collection of legal archives constitutes a genuine revolution in historical legal research because it opens up a wealth of rare and previously inaccessible sources in legal, constitutional, administrative, political, cultural, intellectual, and social history. This unique collection consists of three extensive archives that provide insight into more than 300 years of American and British history. These collections include:

Legal Treatises, 1800-1926: over 20,000 legal treatises provide a comprehensive collection in legal history, business and economics, politics and government.

Trials, 1600-1926: nearly 10,000 titles reveal the drama of famous, infamous, and obscure courtroom cases in America and the British Empire across three centuries.

Primary Sources, 1620-1926: includes reports, statutes and regulations in American history, including early state codes, municipal ordinances, constitutional conventions and compilations, and law dictionaries.

These archives provide a unique research tool for tracking the development of our modern legal system and how it has affected our culture, government, business – nearly every aspect of our everyday life. For the first time, these high-quality digital scans of original works are available via print-on-demand, making them readily accessible to libraries, students, independent scholars, and readers of all ages.

The BiblioLife Network

This project was made possible in part by the BiblioLife Network (BLN), a project aimed at addressing some of the huge challenges facing book preservationists around the world. The BLN includes libraries, library networks, archives, subject matter experts, online communities and library service providers. We believe every book ever published should be available as a high-quality print reproduction; printed on-demand anywhere in the world. This insures the ongoing accessibility of the content and helps generate sustainable revenue for the libraries and organizations that work to preserve these important materials.

The following book is in the "public domain" and represents an authentic reproduction of the text as printed by the original publisher. While we have attempted to accurately maintain the integrity of the original work, there are sometimes problems with the original work or the micro-film from which the books were digitized. This can result in minor errors in reproduction. Possible imperfections include missing and blurred pages, poor pictures, markings and other reproduction issues beyond our control. Because this work is culturally important, we have made it available as part of our commitment to protecting, preserving, and promoting the world's literature.

GUIDE TO FOLD-OUTS MAPS and OVERSIZED IMAGES

The book you are reading was digitized from microfilm captured over the past thirty to forty years. Years after the creation of the original microfilm, the book was converted to digital files and made available in an online database.

In an online database, page images do not need to conform to the size restrictions found in a printed book. When converting these images back into a printed bound book, the page sizes are standardized in ways that maintain the detail of the original. For large images, such as fold-out maps, the original page image is split into two or more pages

Guidelines used to determine how to split the page image follows:

• Some images are split vertically; large images require vertical and horizontal splits.
• For horizontal splits, the content is split left to right.
• For vertical splits, the content is split from top to bottom.
• For both vertical and horizontal splits, the image is processed from top left to bottom right.

A GIFT TO POSTERITY

ON

THE LAWS OF EVQAF

BY

OMER HILMI EFFENDI,

Formerly President of the Civil Temyiz Court,

TRANSLATED BY

C. R. TYSER,

President of the District Court of Kyrenia,

AND

D. G. DEMETRIADES,

Registrar of the District Court of Kyrenia.

SECOND EDITION.

REVISED BY
SIR CHARLES TYSER, CHIEF JUSTICE OF CYPRUS, AND AHMED RAIK EFFENDI,
CHIEF CLERK OF THE LAND REGISTRY OFFICE, KYRENIA,
WITH NOTES BY OMER HILMI IN THE APPENDIX
TRANSLATED BY AHMED RAIK EFFENDI.

CYPRUS:
PRINTED AT THE GOVERNMENT PRINTING OFFICE, NICOSIA.
1922.

THE LAWS OF EVQAF.

A GIFT TO POSTERITY

ON

THE LAWS OF EVQAF

BY

OMER HILMI EFFENDI,

Formerly President of the Civil Temyiz Court,

TRANSLATED BY

C. R. TYSER,

President of the District Court of Kyrenia,

AND

D. G. DEMETRIADES,

Registrar of the District Court of Kyrenia.

SECOND EDITION.

REVISED BY

SIR CHARLES TYSER, CHIEF JUSTICE OF CYPRUS, AND AHMED RAIK EFFENDI,
CHIEF CLERK OF THE LAND REGISTRY OFFICE, KYRENIA,
WITH NOTES BY OMER HILMI IN THE APPENDIX
TRANSLATED BY AHMED RAIK EFFENDI.

CYPRUS:

PRINTED AT THE GOVERNMENT PRINTING OFFICE, NICOSIA.

1922.

INTRODUCTION

FROM THE TURKISH ORIGINAL.

IN ancient times all vaqfs were administered according to the precedents of the Fiqh. After the year 1020 A.H. (A.D. 1610) a law was enacted which was called Ijaretein Law. This law was compiled, as far as possible, according to the principles of the Sheri'. Until the year 1020 A.H. the vaqf Mustaghelat were administered according to the Sheri' usages governing Ijare-i-Vahide and Muqata'a-i-Zemin, but after that date the practice of Ijaretein was introduced. Afterwards many illegal things were done contrary to the principles of the Sacred Law. As a natural evil consequence of the practice of Ijaretein, 120 years after the date above mentioned, the illegal practice of Ghedik was gradually introduced, and therefrom the rights of the old vaqfs were to a great extent injured, and the tenure of vaqf properties was confused.

After the introduction of the practices of Ijaretein and Ghedik in the manner above mentioned many customs and usages came into existence regarding them. These customs and usages were, after being sanctioned by Imperial Irades, recorded in the books of the Courts and the Government offices. But as they were not put in a book, in order to acquire knowledge as to the practices and usages of vaqfs it was necessary to occupy oneself for many years with the affairs of vaqf, and to study the books of the Courts and the records of the Government offices.

I have collected and written the ancient laws and also the customs and usages introduced afterwards relating to vaqf after many years of service in the offices of the Sheykh-ul-Islam, and after obtaining practice in the affairs of Evqaf during a period of nearly twelve years when I acted as the Secretary and Inspector of the Court of Teftish, and also as the Sheri' officer for Public titles. I have collected them among the rules written down in the books of the Fiqh relating to Evqaf, upon which fetwas are given, also I have put together those usages relating to Evqaf which are now acted upon. Therefore I have written a book containing both the rules of the Fiqh and also the laws and usages. To this book I have given the name of "A Gift to Posterity on the Laws of Evqaf."

B

INTRODUCTION

By the Translators.

A.—Vaqf properties are divided into three classes according to the objects for which the property is made vaqf :
(1). Properties made vaqf for religious purposes.
(2). Properties made vaqf for the public benefit.
(3). Customary vaqfs.

(a). Religious vaqf properties include establishments for divine worship—such as vaqf mesjids, &c., and immovable properties of which the income has been directed to be expended on the support of such religious establishments, and which has been made vaqf for that purpose. Also schools and their libraries and religious books, etc., given as vaqf to the different establishments.

(b). Properties made vaqf for the public benefit include hospitals, wells, fountains, bridges, poor-houses, &c.

(c). Customary vaqfs consist of immovable property bought at a low price by some Jami (a consecrated Mosque). By the sale the owner transfers to the Jami his ownership of the immovable property for the price agreed, but he continues to enjoy the property, paying a yearly rent proportional to the price given (see Sakopoulou Mussulmanikon Dikaion, ed. 1871, Vol. II., p. 136, extracted from Belins).

The learned author suggests that the object of owners of land in turning it into customary vaqf land was to escape the liability of its being seized in execution of a judgment.

By the Laws of 21 Ramazan, 1288, and 15 Sheval, 1288, the sale for debt of Mussaqafat and Mustaghelat Mevquf possessed in Ijaretein was allowed.

And now by the Code of Civil Procedure, 1885, the sale of all immovable property is permitted in Cyprus.

As to the power of the Mutevelli to acquire property by purchase or exchange, see Arts. 55, 70, 90, 119, 416, 420.

The Mutevelli cannot buy Arazi mirié or Mevquf or Ijaretein property (Art. 330).

B.—Vaqf lands are divided into two sorts according to the way in which the dedication is made :
(1). Sahiha vaqf lands.—True vaqf lands.
(2). Lands which belong to the Takhsisat category of vaqfs (Art. 124) (see Land Code, Art. 4).

Takhsisat vaqf lands are lands taken from the State lands (Arazi mirié) and made vaqf by special acts of dedication (Takhsis) by the Sultan or by his permission (Land Code, Sec. 4).

The special act of dedication is a true Takhsis, if it consists of the dedication of part of the income belonging to the Beit-ul-mal for the benefit of some object supported by the Beit-ul-mal.

A special dedication of part of the income belonging to the Beit-ul-mal for the benefit of an object not supported by the Beit-ul-mal is an untrue Takhsis (Art. 138).

An untrue Takhsis can be revoked at the will of the Sultan (Art. 138).

As to what vaqfs are vaqfs of the Takhsisat category see Arts. 131, 132, 134 and 137.

Arazi mirié made vaqf of the Takhsisat category is of three kinds :

(1). Land of which only the taxes and tithes are dedicated.

(2). Land of which only the possession is dedicated.

(3). Land of which the possession, taxes and tithes are dedicated (Art. 137).

Sahiha or real vaqfs are vaqfs made by the owners of property in the way described in this law.

The rules contained in Chapter I. deal with the making of real vaqfs.

As to who can make one, see Arts. 43, 51, 53 (2), 55 (2), 56, 57 and 63.

As to how a valid dedication is made, see Arts. 44, 45, 47, 48, 49, 54, 65, 66, 67, 68, 69, 70, 86 and 88.

As to what may be made vaqf, see Arts. 43, 46, 58, 59, 60, 61 62, 63, 64, 65, 66, 72, 73, 81, 82, 83, 84, 85, 87 and 91.

As to what may be objects of vaqfs, see Arts. 71, 74, 75, 76, 77, 78, 79 and 89.

C.—Vaqf immovable properties are divided into four classes according to the way in which the Mutevelli is permitted to deal with them :

(1). Immovable properties which the Mutevelli is not required to let and which may be used by the beneficiaries.

(2). Immovable properties which are directed to be let at a double rent (Ijaretein).

(3). Immovable properties which are to be leased for a fixed term at a single rent (Vahide).

(4). Lands on which there is mulk property belonging to private persons, which are to be let at a single rent (Muqata'a).

1. The most important of the vaqfs of the first class are the Muessesati Khairiye. The law as to them is contained in Arts. 179—186, 343, 344.

If an Ijaretein vaqf is turned into a vaqf of this category it must be turned into a Muqata'alu vaqf (Art. 286).

2. The Law as to Ijareteinle vaqf is dealt with in Chapter VI.—Secs. I. and II., Inheritance; Secs. III., IV., V., VI., VII. and VIII., Alienation; Sec. IX., Partition, etc.; Sec. X.. Rights of owners in common; Sec. XI., Mortgage; Sec. XII., Agents to sell and buy; Sec. XIII., Miscellaneous.

Most of these provisions deal with the rights of the Ijaretein tenant, as owner, to deal with the property.

The relation between the Ijaretein tenant and the vaqf is also dealt with (*see* especially Arts. 187, 188, 192, 263—269, 286 and the articles dealing with alienation and mortgage).

3. The law as to Vahidelu vaqfs is dealt with in Chapter VII.

4. The law as to Muqata'alu vaqfs is dealt with in Chapter VIII.

The law of inheritance depends upon whether it is a real vaqf or one of the Takhsisat category. In the former case only, sons and daughters inherit. In the latter case the law dealing with Arazi mirié applies (Art. 385).

D.—Vaqfs are divided into three classes according to the way in which they are administered.

    (1). Evqaf-i-Mazbuta.—Vaqfs administered directly by the Minister of Evqaf.

        They consist of—

        (*a*). Properties made vaqf by the Sultans and their relations.

        (*b*). Vaqfs of which the Mutevelliship is vacant (Art. 33).

    (2). Evqaf Mulhaqa.—Vaqfs administered by special Mutevellis under the supervision of the Minister of Evqaf (Art. 34).

    (3). Mustesna Evqaf.—Vaqfs managed solely by special Mutevellis without the interference of the Minister of Evqaf. They are dedications made by conquerors and other honourable persons (Art. 35).

The manner of administration of the vaqf depends, in general, upon the terms of the dedication as expressed in the vaqfieh.

The interpretation of the terms used by the dedicator and the construction of the vaqfieh are treated of in Sections I. and II. of Chapter IV. and Section IV. of Chapter I. and Arts. 175, 176, 177.

As to when the term of the dedication need not be observed is treated of in Section III., Chapter IV.

The Mutevelli is the principal officer for the administration of the affairs of the vaqf.

The appointment of the Mutevelli is treated of in Section I., Chapter I. His dismissal in Section III. Chapter I.

The appointment of a substitute for the Mutevelli in Section II., Chapter I.

The Mutevelli may grant his post to another (Art. 306).

The Mutevelli can resign his office (Art. 324).

The duties, powers and liabilities of the Mutevelli are treated of in Chapter X.

If there is more than one Mutevelli, all must consent to any act which is done (Art. 327).

If there is a Nazir the Mutevelli must get his consent (Art. 328). Where the law requires it, he must apply to the judge (Art. 326).

The Mutevelli may appoint an agent (Art. 329).

He must generally follow the directions of the dedicator (Art. 165). He must obtain the leave of the judge if he wish to act otherwise (Art. 165).

When the intention of the dedicator is not known, the Mutevelli must follow the custom (Art. 168). As to where there is no custom see Art. 169.

Sometimes, when the terms of the vaqfieh have not been acted upon from the beginning, they are not to be followed (Art. 170, 171).

As to mistake in the vaqfieh see Art. 172.

The rights of the beneficiaries and the duties of the Mutevellis in respect of them are set out in Chapter XI. and XII.

> With reference to these rights it may be pointed out that the Muajele (rent paid in advance) of an Ijaretein vaqf is regarded as income (Art. 269), and that the expenses of repairs take precedence of grants (Art. 411).

That a beneficiary does not lose his right by abandoning it, but he does by refusing to accept it (Art. 174).

As to rights of persons entitled to inhabit vaqf property (Art. 404, 409—412.)

The following provisions are also important: As to alterations in vaqf property (Art. 267). Building on a vaqf site (Art. 268). Letting vahide land at Muqata'a rent (Art. 274). Letting vahide land at Ijaretein (Art. 275). As to the irrevocability of a dedication see Arts. 111, 114, 119, and 120. As to dedicated money (Art. 350).

In making this translation the translators have derived great assistance from the Greek translation of Mr. Nicolaides and from the help of Ismail Hakki Effendi, Turkish Clerk in the District Court of Kyrenia and formerly Clerk in the Daavi Court.

CONTENTS.

PREFACE.

Part I.—Arts. 1—32. Definitions of terms in Sacred Law.
  „ II.—Arts. 33—42.   „   „   Civil   „

CHAPTER I.

Sec. I.—Constituent elements of dedication, Arts. 43—55
  „ II.—Validity of dedication, Arts. 53 (2)—80
  „ III.—   „   „   Arts. 81—93
  „ IV.—Dedication, what is included, Arts. 94—98
  „ V.—Dedication by sick persons, Arts. 99—110

CHAPTER II.

Sec. I.—Irrevocability of dedication, Arts. 111—118
  „ II.—Rules relating to revocability, Arts. 119—123.

CHAPTER III.

Dedicated Lands, Arts. 124—139

CHAPTER IV.

Sec. I.—Interpretation, Arts. 140—160
  „ II.—Power to alter dedication, Arts. 161—164
  „ III.—When terms of dedication not obligatory, Arts. 165—177

CHAPTER V.

Different sorts of dedicated properties, Arts. 178—186
Pious establishments (muessesati khairiye). Arts. 179—186

CHAPTER VI.

Ijaretein vaqfs, Arts. 187—269
Sec. I.—Inheritance, Arts. 187—192
  „ II.—Disabilities of heirs, Arts. 193—197
  „ III.—Alienation, Arts. 198—208
  „ IV.—   „   by sick person, Arts. 209—213
  „ V.—   „   by a guardian, Arts. 214—217
  „ VI.—   „   conditional, Arts. 218, 219
  „ VII.—   „   options, Arts. 220—222
  „ VIII.—Price and recovery, Arts. 223—226
  „ IX.—Partition, etc., Arts. 227—239
  „ X.—Ijaretein vaqfs held in common, Arts. 240—243
  „ XI.—Mortgage, Arts. 244—254
  „ XII.—Agents to sell or buy, Arts. 255—262
  „ XIII.—Miscellaneous, Arts. 263—269

CHAPTER VII.

Ijare-i-Vahide vaqfs, Arts. 270—275

CHAPTER VIII.

Muqata'alu vaqfs, Arts. 276—286

CHAPTER IX.

Mutevelli, Arts. 287—325
Sec. I.—Appointment of Mutevelli, Arts. 287—302
  ,, II.—   ,,   Qaimaqam-i-Mutevelli, Arts. 303—307
  ,, III.—Accounts of Mutevelli, Arts. 308—312
  ,, IV.—Dismissal of Mutevelli, Arts. 313—325

CHAPTER X.

Things done by the Mutevelli, Arts. 326—355
Sec. I.—For what acts Mutevelli liable in damages Arts.
          226—333
  ,, II.—Compromise and release of debt by Mutevelli,
          Arts. 334—336
  ,, III.—Mutevelli's liability as bailee, proof of accounts,
          Arts. 337—339
  ,, IV.—When Mutevelli may spend money of one trust
          on another, Arts. 340—342
  ,, V.—Useless charitable institutions, Arts. 343, 344
  ,, VI.—Borrowing powers of Mutevelli, Arts. 345—349
  ,, VII.—Dedicated money, Arts. 350—355

CHAPTER XI.

Grants from dedicated properties, Arts. 356—371

CHAPTER XII.

Appointments in reference to trusts, Arts. 372—382
Sec. I.—The giving of appointments, Arts. 372—379
  ,, II.—Deputation and discontinuance of office, Arts.
          380—382

CHAPTER XIII.

Letting of vaqf properties, Arts. 383—401

CHAPTER XIV.

Trespass against vaqfs, Arts. 402—408

CHAPTER XV.

Repairs and buildings in relation to vaqfs, Arts. 409—415
Sec. I.—Repairs by beneficiary entitled to occupy, Arts.
          409—413
  ,, II.—Buildings raised on vaqf land, Arts. 414, 415

CHAPTER XVI.

Exchange of dedicated property, Arts. 416—420

CHAPTER XVII.

Actions relating to vaqfs, Arts. 421—449
Sec. I.—When an action can be brought, Arts. 421—434
 ,, II.—Prescription, Arts. 435—449

CHAPTER XVIII.

Parties to actions, Arts. 450—461

CHAPTER XIX.

Evidence, Arts. 462—475
Sec. I.—Admissibility of evidence, Arts. 462—467
 ,, II.—Hearsay evidence, Arts. 468, 469
 ,, III.—Burden of Proof, Arts. 470—475

CHAPTER XX.

Oath of Mutevelli, Arts. 476, 477

CHAPTER XXI.

Admission, Arts, 478—482

APPENDIX

INDEX

GLOSSARY

OF TECHNICAL AND OTHER TERMS USED IN THE BOOK.

Adi (عادى)—Customary (Art. 41).

Ahfad (احفاد)—Grandchildren (Art. 22).

Arazi Kharajié (اراضئ خراجيه)—One sort of Mulk land, being land left at the time of the conquest in the hands of non-Mussulman owners (Land Code, Art. 2). On the death of the owner without heirs it belongs to the Beit-ul-mal and becomes subject to the same law as Arazi mirié.

Arazi Mevat (اراضئ موات)—Unowned waste land (*see* Land Code, Art. 6).

Arazi Memluke (اراضئ مملوك)—Land possessed absolutely, land held in fee simple. There are four sorts :

    1. Building sites within a town or village and places on the borders of towns or villages, considered necessary to complete a habitation, being at most half a donum in extent.

    2. Land separated from Arazi mirié and made Mulk in the manner hereinafter described.

    3. Arazi Ushrie.

    4. Arazi Kharajié.

Arazi mirié (اراضئ ميريه)—A class of lands, the raqabe of which belongs to the Beit-ul-mal, and of which the transfer and grant of possession is carried out by the government.

Arazi Ushrie (اراضئ عشريه)—Land given and distributed at the time of the conquest to those who had seized it. On the death of the owner without heirs it belongs to the Beit-ul-mal and becomes subject to the same law as Arazi mirié.

Avariz Vaqfi (عوارض وقفى)—Vaqf for the poor of a neighbourhood (Art. 36).

Bedeli Feragh (بدل فراغ)—Money consideration for a sale (Art. 17).

Beit-ul-mal (بيت المال)—Government Treasury.

Berat (برات)—Commission, Letters Patent.

Bey' (بيع)—Sale in accordance with Sheri' law.

Bezestan (بزستان)—A covered market place for the sale of valuable things.

Chiftlik (جفتلك)—A farm.

Defter Khaqani (دفترخاقانى)—The office where the real estate registers are kept.

Djihet—See Jihet.

Ehli Vezaif (اهل وظائف)—People who receive salary and victuals from a vaqf (Art. 21).

Evlad-i-Sulbieh (اولاد صلبيه)—Children (Art. 23).

Evqaf (اوقاف)—Plural of vaqf (Art. 2).

Evqaf-i-Mazbuta (اوقاف مضبوطه)—Vaqfs administered directly by the Minister of Evqaf (Art. 33).

Evqaf-i-Mulhaqa (اوقاف ملحقه)—Vaqfs administered by a special trustee under the supervision of the Minister of Evqaf.

Evqaf-i-Mustesna (مستثنى اوقاف)—Vaqfs administered by special trustees without the supervision of the Minister of Evqaf.

Faqir (فقير)—Poor.

Farigh (فارغ)—The alienor of property (Art. 17).

Feragh (فراغ)—Alienation of property (Art. 17).

Feragh bedeli (بدل فراغ)—Money consideration for alienation (Art. 17)

Feragh bil vefa (فراغ بالوفا)—Mortgage (Art. 19).

Feragh-i-qati' (فراغ قطعى)—Final alienation (Art. 18).

Ghedik (كدك)—Tools, etc., on vaqfs (Art. 40).

Ghairi Lazim (غير لازم)—Revocable (Art. 4).

Ghalle-i-vaqf (غنة وقف)—The income of a vaqf (Art. 5).

Hajj (حج)—A pilgrimage.

Hanefi (حنفى)—Of the Hanefi Sect.

Haremein-i-Sherifein (حرمين شريفين)—The Holy Cities—Mecca, Medina.

Hujjet (حجت)—A title-deed.

Huquq (حقوق)—Rights, appurtenances of real property.

Ijare (اجاره)—Rent.

Ijare-i-misl (اجارة مثل)—Equivalent rent, rent equal to the value to let of the property.

Ijaretein (اجارتين)—Two rents (Art. 35).

Ijareteinlu (اجارتينلو)—With payment of Ijaretein.

Ijare-i-Vahide (اجارة واحده)—One rent (Art. 38).

Ijare-i-Vahidelu Evqaf (اجارة واحدهلو اوقاف)—Evqaf let at a single rent (Art. 38).

'Ilam (اعلام)—Judgment of a Sheri' Court.

Imam (امام)—A leader in prayer.

Imarat (عمارات)—Poorhouses, soup kitchens.

Intiqal (انتقال)—Inheritance, succession.

Istibdal (استبدال)—Exchange (Art. 31).

Istiglal (استغلال)—A mortgage with the condition that the mortgagor should become tenant of the mortgagee (Art. 20).

Jabi-i-Vaqf (جابئ وقف)—The collector of the income of the vaqf (Art. 12).

Jami (جامع)—A mosque.

Jihat (جهات)—Plural of Jihet (Art. 372).

Jihet (جهة)—A vaqf appointment (Art. 372).

Khademe (خدمه)—Servant, Officer.

Khairat (خيرات)—Pious foundations.

Kharaj (خراج)—Tax.

Kharajié (خراجيه)—*See* Arazi Kharajié.

Lazim (لازم)—Irrevocable (Art. 4).

Mahlul (محلول)—Escheat, lapse.

Mal-i-Muteqavvim (مال متقوم)—A thing of which the use is lawful and the possession has been acquired Art. 46).

Mazbata (مضبطه)—The judgment of a Civil Court.

Mazbuta (مضبوطه)—*See* Evqaf Mazbuta.

Mefrugh bih (مفروغ به)—A vaqf property alienated (Art. 17).

Mefrugh leh (مفروغ له)—The grantee of a vaqf property alienated (Art. 17).

Meremet-i-ghairi Mustehlike (رمت غير مستهلكه)—Work on a house which can be separated (Art. 30).

Meremet-i-Mustehlike (رمت مستهلكه)—Work on a house which cannot be separated, *e.g.* painting (Art. 29).

Meshrutun leh (مشروط له)—Beneficiaries (Art. 7).

Mesjid (مسجد)—A small mosque.

Mevat (موات)—A class of waste land (Land Code, Art. 6).

Mevquf (موقوف)—Dedicated (Art. 1).

Mevqufun aleih (موقوف عليه)—Beneficiary (Art. 7).

Mirié (ميريه)—*See* Arazi mirié.

Muajele (معجله)—Rent in advance (Art. 187).

Muejele (مؤجله)—Rent paid afterwards (Art. 187).

Muessesati Khairiye (مؤسسات خيريه)—Philanthropic establishments, charitable institutions (Art. 16).

Muhassebeji (حاسبجي)—Accountant.

Mujtehid (مجتهد)—A recognized jurisconsult (note to Art. 111).

Mulhaqa (ملحقه)—*See* Evqaf Mulhaqa.

Mulk (ملك)—Ownership in fee simple, property owned in fee simple.

Multezim (ملتزم)—Revenue or tithe farmer.

Munqati' el akhir (منقطع الاخر)—A vaqf the beneficiary of which ceases to exist (Art. 78).

Munqati' el evdel (مقطع الاول)—A vaqf the beneficiary of which does not exist at the beginning (Art. 77).

Munqati' el wasat (مقطع اوسط)—A vaqf the beneficiary of which ceases to exist for a time (Art. 79).

Muqata'a (مقاطعه)—The annual rent paid for vaqf land on which there are mulk buildings, &c.

Muqata'alu (مقاطعه‌لو)—With payment of Muqata'a rent; also written Muqata'ale.

Murtezika (مرتزقه)—Beneficiaries (Art. 21).

Mussaqaf (مسقف)—A roofed building from which income is derived (Art. 15).

Mussaqafat (مسقفات)—Plural of Mussaqaf (Art. 15).

Mustaghel (مستغل)—Property capable of beneficial possession. Income bearing property (Art. 14).

Mustaghelat (مستغلات)—Plural of Mustaghel (Art. 14).

Muste'jir (مستأجر)—A person who hires (Mejellé, Art. 410).

Mustesna Evqaf (مستثنى اوقاف)—*See* Evqaf-i-Mustesna.

Mutasarrif (متصرف)—The tenant of Arazi mirié and Ijareteinlu vaqf.

Mutekellimun'ala el vaqf (متكلم على الوقف)—Means Mutevelli (Art. 9).

Mutevelli (متولى)—The trustee of a vaqf (Art. 8).

Naqshbendi (نقشبندى)—An order of Dervishes.

Nazaret (نظارت)—The office of Nazir.

Nazir Vaqf (ناظر وقف)—The person who overlooks the Mutevelli (Art. 11).

Nesl (نسل)—Lawful children and grandchildren (Art. 24).

Nizamli (نظاملى)—Legal (Art. 41).

Qaimaqam-i-Mutevelli (قائمقام متولى)—Substitute for Mutevelli (Art. 10).

Qaim-i-Vaqf (قيم وقف)—Another name for the Mutevelli (Art. 9).

Quvvam (قوام)—Plural of Qaim-i-Vaqf (Art. 9).

Raqabe (رقبه)—The neck, subjection (*see* Tasarruf).

Reshid (رشيد)—A man capable of managing his property (Art. 13).

Rey' (ريع)—The produce of vaqf property (Art. 5).

Rusumat (رسومات)—Duties, tolls.

Sahiha Vaqf (صحيحه وقف)—True vaqf (Art. 124).

Sened (سند)—A title-deed.

Shafi'i (شافى)—The Shafi'i school or sect.

Shazeliye (شاذليه)—Name of the order founded by the Sheykh Shazeli (شيخ شاذلى).

Sheri' (شرع)—Sacred Law.

Sheykh (شيخ)—An elder, head of a tribe, head of a religious community.

Ta'amul (تعامل)—The prevailing use (Art. 27).

Takhsis (تخصيص)—The dedication of a vaqf of the Takhsisat category (Art. 138).

Takhsisat (تخصيصات)—Property of the Beit-ul-mal specially made vaqf (Art. 3).

Tapou (طابو)—The payment made in advance to the Government for the possession of State Land by the person entitled to take the land in making such payment (Land Code, Section 3).

Tasarruf (تصرف)—This word denotes the rights of the possessor (mutasarrif) of Arazi mirié and Ijareteinlu vaqf. Tasarruf and raqabe together constitute full rights of ownership. The owner of mulk has both the tasarruf and the raqabe (Land Code, Art. 2).

Teberru' (تبرع)—Transfer without consideration (Art. 26).

Teberru'at (تبرعات)—Plural of Teberru' (Art. 26).

Tekiye (تكيه)—A convent and chapel of Dervishes, &c.

Temlikname (تمليكنامه)—A document granting State Lands as mulk (Art. 130).

Terike (تركه)—The estate left by a person at his death.

Tesjil-i-istibdal (تسجيل استبدال)—A decision of the validity of an exchange (Art. 32).

Tesjil-i-vaqf (تسجيل وقف)—The deciding that a property is irrevocably dedicated (Art. 6).

Tevliet (توليت)—The office of Mutevelli.

Ulema (علما)—Men learned in Sheri' Law.

Ushrie (عشريه)—*See* Arazi Ushrie.

Vahidelu (واحدلو)—*See* Ijare-i-Vahidelu.

Vaqf (وقف)—The act of dedicating (Art. 1). The thing dedicated (Art. 2).

Vaqfieh (وقفيه)—The Sheri' judgment about a vaqf, containing the terms of the dedication and the decision of the judge upon it (Art. 25).

Vaqif (واقف)—The dedicator (Art. 1).

Vazife (وظيفه)—Salary and food given out of the produce of the Vaqf property (Art. 21).

Vazaif (وظائف)—Plural of Vazife.

Zurriyet (ذريت)—Children and grandchildren (Art. 24).

THE LAWS OF EVQAF.

THIS BOOK WITH A PREFACE CONTAINS 21 CHAPTERS.

PREFACE.

The meanings of technical terms used with reference to Vaqf; it is divided into two parts.

PART I.

The meanings of technical terms connected with Vaqf used in the Sheri' Law.

ARTICLE 1.—" Vaqf " is the tying up of a property itself and the imposition of an interdiction on its transfer in such a way that its benefit is given to men on the condition that the property is to be regarded as the property of God. It is equivalent to " dedication." **Vaqf.**

" Vaqif " is the name given to a person who makes a vaqf. **Vaqif.**

" Mevquf " and " Mahall-i-Vaqf " (Vaqf place) is what the thing itself which is made Vaqf is called. **Mevquf, mahall-i-vaqf.**

ART. 2.—" Vaqf," while it is used in the signification above mentioned, is used also to denote the thing itself made Vaqf. Such a property is Vaqf they say. " Vaqf " makes " Evqaf " in the plural. **Vaqf.** **Evqaf.**

ART. 3.—Vaqf-i-Irsady consists in the appointing by the Padishah of the use of a part of the possessions of the Beit-ul-mal to someone having a claim by the Sheri' Law on the Beit-ul-mal and in a special assignment being made by an order of the Government. **Vaqf-i-Irsady.**

Evqaf made Vaqf by Vaqf-i-Irsady are called Takhsisat. **Takhsisat.**

ART. 4.—Vaqfs are divided into 2 classes: Lazim and Ghairi Lazim. A Lazim Vaqf is one which cannot be annulled. **Lazim and Ghairi Lazim.**

A Vaqf-i-Ghairi Lazim is a Vaqf which can be annulled.

ART. 5.—Ghalle-i-Vaqf denotes the benefit and produce of the dedicated property, such as the interest of dedicated money, the rent of dedicated property and the fruits of a dedicated garden. **Ghalle-i-Vaqf.**

Rey' Vaqf has the same meaning as Ghalle-i-Vaqf. **Rey' Vaqf.**

ART. 6.—Tesjil-i-Vaqf is the giving of a judgment, to be declared, deciding specially upon the condition of a Vaqf that it is irrevocably dedicated (Art. 111, &c.) **Tesjil-i-Vaqf.**

ART. 7.—The object in favour of which the benefits of a Vaqf have been limited and assigned by the dedicator is called Meshrutun leh and Mevqufun aleih and Masraf-i-Vaqf. **Meshrutun leh Mevqufun aleih Masraf-i-Vaqf.**

C

Mutevelli.

ART. 8.—A Mutevelli is a person appointed to supervise and manage, in accordance with the terms of the dedication, the business and affairs of the Vaqf.

Mutevellis are of two kinds:

(1) A Mutevelli according to a stipulation of the Vaqfieh who is required by the terms of the Vaqfieh to be Mutevelli.

(2) A Mutevelli who is appointed by the judge alone, without any direction being given by the dedication for that purpose.

Qaim.

Qowvvam.

Mutekellimun-ala-el-Vaqf.

Qaimaqam-i-Mutevelli.

ART. 9.—Qaim-i-Vaqf is a name given to the Mutevelli of a Vaqf. Plural Qowvvam.

A Mutevelli is also called Mutekellimun-ala-el-Vaqf.

ART. 10.—Qaimaqam-i-Mutevelli is the name given as will hereafter be explained, to the person appointed by the judge as a substitute for the Mutevelli. The person carrying out the duties of the Mutevelli (Art. 380, &c.)

Naziri Vaqf.

ART. 11.—" Naziri Vaqf " is the name given to the person who is appointed to overlook the management of the vaqf property by the Mutevelli and to whom the Mutevelli will refer for his opinion as to the affairs of the vaqf. It is equivalent to Overseer.

In some cities, it is the custom to use the word " Nazaret " for " tevliet." In those towns, the Mutevelli is called also " Naziri Vaqf."

Jabi-i-Vaqf.

ART. 12.—" Jabi-i-Vaqf " is the name given to the person who collects the revenue of the vaqf.

Reshid.

ART. 13.—" Reshid " is a man who has knowledge of affairs, who does not waste his property contrary to the sacred law and good sense (Mejellé, Art. 947).

Mustaghel.

ART. 14.—" Mustaghel," plural " Mustaghelat," is the name given to property dedicated for providing the persons who have the management of philanthropic establishments (Muessesati Khairiye) with the income required. It is either immovable property, such as vineyards, gardens, inns, baths, or movables, such as money given on the condition that it shall be let out at interest, and

Ghedik.

the tools of an artificer called " ghedik."

Mussaqafat.

ART. 15.—" Mussaqaf, " plural " Mussaqafat," means a building from which income is derived and which has a roof (see note).

Muessesati Khairiye.

ART. 16.—" Muessesati Khairiye " is the name given to establishments for the public good, built and dedicated by philanthropic persons ; such as places of religious worship, seminaries, schools, places for feeding the poor, reading rooms, chapels, libraries, places for the maintenance of the poor, guest houses, bridges, hospitals, asylums, fountains, public fountains, tanks, wells, and cemeteries.

ART. 17.—" Feragh " (alienation) with reference to Mustaghelat and Mussaqafat vaqfs consists in the abandoning and granting the right of tasarruf of such properties to another. The person who grants it is called " Farigh." The grantee " Mefrugh Leh "; the dedicated thing granted, " Mefrugh Bih "; the money which the grantor receives as consideration for the grant " Bedeli Feragh." Feragh. Farigh, Mefrugh Leh. Bedeli Feragh.

ART. 18.—" Feragh-i-Qati' " is the grant made without condition. Feragh-i-Qati'.

ART. 19.—" Feragh bil Vefa " when used with reference to Mussaqafat and Mustaghelat Vaqf, is the name given to a grant made to a creditor, in consideration of a sum borrowed, on the condition that the vaqf granted should be given back into the possession of the grantor as soon as the debt is paid: It is equivalent to a grant with right of redemption (Mejellé, Art. 118). Feragh bil Vefa.

ATR. 20.—" Istighlal," with reference to Mussaqafat and Mustaghelat Vaqfs, is the name given to a grant with power of redemption, under the condition that the grantor should hire the thing granted from the grantee (Mejellé, Art. 119). Istighlal.

ART. 21.—" Vazife " is the name given to the salary and victuals given out of the produce of the vaqf, plural " Vazaif." Vazife.

The people who receive the salary and the victuals are called " Murteziqa " and " Ehli Vazaif." Murteziqa. Ehli Vazaif.

ART. 22.—" Ahfad " means " grandchildren." Ahfad.

ART. 23.—" Evlad-i-Sulbieh " is the name given to the children, the direct issue of a person. Therefore the grandchildren of a man may not be so called. Evlad-i-Sulbieh.

ART. 24.—" Nesl " includes children and grandchildren. " Zurriyet " has the same meaning as Nesl. Nesl. Zurriyet.

ART. 25.—" Vaqfieh " is the Sheri' hujjet about a vaqf, in which is contained the declaration of the dedicator about the dedication, and the judicial declaration of its validity. Vaqfieh.

ART. 26.—" Teberru', " plural " Teberru'at," is the transfer of the property in a thing without consideration (Mejellé, Arts. 57 and 833). Teberru'.

ART. 27.—" Ta'amul " is the prevailing use. Thus by the use of two or three persons Ta'amul is not constituted. Ta'amul.

ART. 28.—" Faqir," poor, is one who has not such property as to be required to pay Zekiat (a payment of alms required by law.) Faqir.

Therefore, the person who possesses such property is looked upon by the sacred law as a rich person.

Meremet-i-Mustehlike.

ART. 29.—" Meremet-i-Mustehlike " is the name given to the work done upon a building which cannot be separated from it, such as painting and white-washing.

Meremet-i-ghairi Mustehlike.

ART. 30.—" Meremet-i-ghairi Mustehlike " means such things as can be separated from a building, such as newly added buildings.

Istibdal.

ART. 31.—" Istibdal " is the exchange of a vaqf property for a mulk property.

Tesjil-i-Istibdal.

ART. 32.—" Tesjil-i-Istibdal " is the decision as to the validity of the exchange and its ability to be executed, as a consequence of which, it cannot be set aside.

PART II.

Definitions of terms connected with Vaqfs found in the Civil Law.

Evqaf-i-Mazbuta.

ART. 33.—" Evqaf-i-Mazbuta " is the name given to Vaqf properties administered directly by the Minister of Evqaf.

Evqaf-i-Mazbuta are of two categories :

(1). Evqaf dedicated by their Majesties the Sultans and their Highnesses their relations. Of the above Vaqfs the condition of the dedication was originally that the Mutevelliship should be for the Caliph. The Minister of Evqaf is ordered by the Caliph as his representative, to carry out the duties of the Mutevelliship.

(2). The dedicated properties which are held and administered by the Evqaf Treasury, when the office of Mutevelli, which has been limited by the dedicator in favour of his descendants and his relations, is vacant (*see note*).

Evqaf-i-Mulhaqa.

ART. 34.—Evqaf-i-Mulhaqa " is the name given to dedicated properties which are administered by special Mutevellis under the supervision of the Minister of Evqaf.

Whilst the superintendence of most vaqfs of this sort was appointed originally by the dedicators in favour of the Prime Ministers, the Sheykh-ul-Islams, the Chief Eunuchs, the two Army Judges, the Fetva Emini, the Judges of Constantinople and the three Cities, and the high officials, and was managed by them ; afterwards, when the Ministry of Evqaf was established, their superintendence was given over to it.

The lawfulness of the superintendence of these dedicated properties by the Ministry of Evqaf depends on the authority given by the persons to whom the superintendence was originally given.

Mustesna Evqaf.

ART. 35.—" Mustesna Evqaf," excepted evqaf, are those which are managed solely by special Mutevellis without the interference of the Minister of Evqaf, *e.g.* dedications made by conquerors and other honourable persons.

ART. 36.—"Avariz Vaqfi" is the name given to a dedication, which is founded to provide assistance for the unfortunate and needy inhabitants of a village or neighbourhood ; as, *e.g.* foundations for the burial of the poor who die in some village or quarter, the support of the sick who are unable to earn their livelihood, and for the repair in some village or quarter of the paved aqueducts which need repair. *Avariz Vaqfi.*

ART. 37.—"Ijaretein" means the two rents which are paid, the one in advance and the other at the expiration of a term. *Ijaretein.*

The roofed and income bearing vaqfs which are so rented at double rent are called "Ijareteinlu."

ART. 38.—"Ijare-i-Vahidelu Evqaf" is the name given to Mussaqafat and Mustaghelat vaqfs which are let by the Mutevelli of the dedication, in the same way as properties are let by their owners, for a term, long or short, such as a month or a year. *Ijare-i-Vahidelu Evqaf.*

ART. 39.—"Muqata'a" means the annual rent, which is appointed to be paid for land to the vaqfs, by the person in possession of a property of which the ground is vaqf, and the buildings, trees and vines thereon are Mulk. It is also called "Ijare-i-Zemin," "Rent of Land." *Muqata'a. Ijare-i-Zemin.*

ART. 40.—"Ghedik" is the name given to the tools of a special trade guild or art, placed on a property permanently established (*see* 8 Zilhijje, 1277). *Ghedik.*

ART. 41.—Some of the dedicated ghediks are called "Nizamli" (legal) and some are called "'adi" (customary). *Nizamli, adi.*

ART. 42.—"Nizamli Ghedikiati Mevqufe" are from the sacred vaqfs of the glorious ancestor of the Sultan, Mahmoud Khan and of the two sacred towns.

All the other ghediks of vaqfs are called "'adi."

Mention will be made of the difference between legal and customary ghediks in the chapter on sale with power of redemption of the heading "Ijaretein."

CHAPTER I.

(1) The completion and motive of the dedication ; (2) the conditions of its validity, and (3) certain rules.

SECTION I.

The completion and motive of the dedication.

What may be dedicated.
Dedicator must have legal capacity.

ART. 43.—A dedicated thing must consist of a thing capable of the consequences of the dedication and the dedication must be made by a person having legal capability as regards the constituent elements of the dedication (Mejellé, Arts. 361, 363 and 859).

Words of dedication.

ART. 44.—A constituent element of the dedication is the expressions which constitute the dedication, such as " I dedicated my property," or "I gave it as permanent charity," (Mejellé, 838), *see* Arts. 54, 55.

Dedication by signs.

ART. 45.—A dedication can also be made by the known signs of a dumb person (Mejellé, Art. 174).

Thing dedicated must be one of which the use is lawful and of which the property has been acquired.

ART. 46.—A thing in order that it may be capable of dedication must be " Mal-i-Muteqavvim."

The term " Mal-i-Muteqavvim " is used to denote a thing of which the use is lawful and a thing of which the possession has been acquired.

In the foregoing subject it is taken in both senses (Mejellé, Art. 127).

Acceptance when necessary.

ART. 47.—The acceptance of the thing dedicated is not required at the time when the dedication is made if the beneficiaries are undefined persons.

Consequently in such a case the dedication is constituted by the proposal alone of the dedicator, *e.g.*, if a person dedicating his property limits the benefit of it in favour of the poor of some city, the completion of the dedication does not depend upon the acceptance of the poor of that city.

But if the persons in whose favour the dedication is made are determined, the completion of the dedication depends on their acceptance.

A man who refuses to accept a dedication made in his favour, prevents the constitution of the dedication only so far as it benefits himself ; that is to say, he is deprived of the benefit granted out of the thing dedicated.

He does not prevent the constitution of the dedication in favour of others ; *e.g.*, when someone has dedicated his property and has limited the income thereof in favour of his son and after him to the poor of some zaviye, this son, if he does not accept the thing dedicated, deprives himself only of the income of the thing dedicated and its income belongs to the poor of that zaviye (Mejellé, Art. 837).

ART. 48.—The silence of the person in whose favour the dedication is made is looked upon as an implied consent. *[Silence gives consent.]*

Consequently, if the person in whose favour the dedication is made keeps silent, not saying anything which shews whether he accepts or refuses to accept the dedication, his silence is looked upon as an implied acceptance and he acquires a right to the benefit of the thing dedicated (Mejellé, Art. 67).

ART. 49.—An acceptance made after refusal, and a refusal after acceptance are invalid. *[Acceptance or refusal is final.]*

Therefore if a person in whose favour a dedication is made, after having refused it, change his mind and accept the dedication, he does not acquire a right to the benefit of the thing dedicated. Also if after the acceptance of a dedication, the person in whose favour it is made reject it his rejection is invalid and he is not deprived of the benefit which belongs to him under the terms expressed by the dedicator.

ART. 50.—The consequence of a dedication is that the thing dedicated itself is made inalienable and its benefit is given to men. *[Consequence of dedication.]*

ART. 51.—In order that a person may make a dedication, the law requires that he should be free, of sound mind, and of full age (Mejellé 859) *see* Arts. 53 (2), 55 (2). *[Legal capacity to dedicate.]*

ART. 52.—The motive of dedication is the seeking to approach God and worship Him by the gift of property for philanthropic purposes. *[Motive of dedication.]*

ART. 53.—The most acceptable of dedications, is the dedication of a thing of which men have the greatest need, *e.g.* the erection and dedication of a school in a place where there are sufficient fountains for the wants of the inhabitants is more acceptable and charitable than the erection of a fountain. *[What dedications are the better.]*

ART. 54.—If a person buy a thing with the intention of founding a dedication, but say nothing to shew that he dedicated the thing after he bought it, the dedication is not constituted by the mere intention. *[An intention to dedicate does not alone effect a dedication.]*

ART. 55.—If the Mutevelli of a Vaqf buy something on account of the vaqf out of the income of the vaqf, this thing does not become vaqf by the mere fact that it has been purchased out of the income of the vaqf. *[Of things purchased with the income or principal of dedicated property.]*

Therefore the Mutevelli can, with the consent of the vendor, annul the sale or sell that thing to another.

But if the Mutevelli has, after the purchase, limited the thing, in accordance with the law, by a decree of the judge, for the benefit of the vaqf, then the thing becomes vaqf.

But if the Mutevelli does not buy the said thing with the income of the vaqf, and acquires it by the expenditure of the thing originally dedicated, in such a case that thing becomes vaqf by the mere purchase.

E.g. If the Mutevelli buy a property with dedicated money appointed to be converted into property, such property becomes vaqf by the mere purchase.

For this, the consecration of the dedication by the decision of the judge is not necessary.

SECTION II.

Conditions of the validity and invalidity of dedications.

Validity of dedications.

Dedicator must have mental capacity.

ART. 53 (2).—It is necessary that the dedicator should be capable of making a transfer of ownership and of doing acts of charity.

Therefore dedications made by infants, lunatics and persons who have arrived at their second childhood are not valid.

The dedication, however, of anything for their benefit is valid.

Must be free.

The dedication made by a person who is not free is also invalid.

Unless with special permission.

But a slave may validly make a dedication after he has obtained his master's permission to dedicate a defined thing (Mejellé, Art. 859).

Free will.

ART. 54 (2).—The consent of the dedicator is required.

Therefore a dedication, induced by what is force according to law, is not valid (Mejellé, Arts. 949 and 1003, 1007, 860).

Dedicator must not be inhibited.

ART. 55 (2).—The dedicator must be a man who has not been inhibited for debt or extravagance.

Therefore the dedication of an extravagant person or debtor, who has been inhibited, made before the inhibition has been removed, is invalid (Mejellé, Arts. 990, 998).

Dedicator need not be a subject of a Mahomedan state.

ART. 56.—It is not necessary that the dedicator should be a subject of a Mahomedan country.

Thus a dedication made by a foreigner in a Mahomedan country is valid.

Dedicator and beneficiary need not be of the same religion.

ART. 57.—It is not necessary that the dedicator and the person in whose favour the dedication is made should belong to the same religion.

Therefore if a Mussulman limits the benefit of a thing which he dedicates in favour of non-Mussulman poor or a non-Mussulman limits the benefit of a thing he dedicates in favour of Mussulman poor, the dedication is valid and the condition is of force.

Thing dedicated must be immovable property.

ART. 58.—It is necessary that the thing dedicated be immovable property.

Therefore the dedication of independent movable property is not valid.

But if there is a prevailing custom in a town, that certain movable properties may be dedicated, the dedication in that town of such movable property is valid. *E.g.*, the dedication of books and works and of the holy Koran and Delail in order that those who wish may study and read them, of money lent at interest in order that the interest thereof may be expended for philanthropic purposes, of furniture and copper utensils to be used in schools, seminaries and philanthropic establishments, of clothes and ornaments to be lent for use of brides at weddings, of animals such as sheep, goats and cows, that their produce may belong to some philanthropical object and of seed to be lent to poor farmers who have no seed, is valid. *Unless custom to dedicate movable property.*

ART. 59.—The dedication of movable property subject to immovable property is valid. *Movable property as subject to immovable may be dedicated.*

That is to say, where immovable property is dedicated, the dedication with it of movable property, subject to it, is valid, whether a custom exists that such movable property may be dedicated, or not.

E.g. Where a chiftlik is dedicated, the movable things found upon the chiftlik and subject to it, such as agricultural implements and seed, can be validly dedicated with the chiftlik as subject to it (Mejellé, Art. 54).

ART. 60.—The thing dedicated must be the thing itself. *Thing dedicated must be the thing itself, not a chose in action.*

The dedication therefore of a debt owing by someone before payment is not valid.

Consequently where someone has dedicated for a defined purpose a sum of money, which he is entitled to receive from another person, he can spend the same, after recovery from the debtor, for his own purposes, he can also give a valid release for the debt, also if he dedicates the same and dies before receiving or acquitting the debt, the heirs can receive the same from the debtor and include it in the inheritance for the purpose of distributing it among themselves.

In such a case, the Mutevelli of the dedication cannot bring an action claiming this money by reason of its having been dedicated in the manner mentioned.

But a man can validly bequeath a sum of money due to him for the purpose of its being dedicated to a philanthropic object. In such a case if he dies before receiving the loan from the debtor, it is regarded as already having been dedicated, and belongs to the charity designated, when recovered from the debtor, if it does not exceed a third of the estate. *Exception in case of bequests.*

Also the dedication only of the benefit derived from immovable property, without the property itself, is not valid. *Not the income alone from property.*

E.g. If a person dedicates only the income and rent derived from his house to a philanthropic object and reserves for himself the ownership of the house, the dedication is not valid.

Grant of income sometimes construed as grant of corpus.

But if any one says, that he grants the income of a certain property of his, as alms to be given in perpetuity to the poor necessarily then it is considered that that property has been dedicated for the benefit of the poor.

A thing may be dedicated although others have rights over it.

ART. 61.—It is not an indispensable condition that there should be no claim by a third person to the thing dedicated.

Consequently an immovable property mortgaged or let to a third person can be validly dedicated for any object. Nevertheless, the mortgage or lease is not invalidated in consequence of such dedication.

The property belongs to the establishment for the benefit of which it was dedicated, in the second case at the expiration of the term of the lease, or when it is rescinded by the death of one of the contracting parties or by the consent of the parties, and in the first case when the mortgage is cancelled.

But if the dedicator dies before paying his debt to the mortgagee, the following rules are observed :—

If the dedicator has other property, besides that dedicated, sufficient to pay the debt, the debt to the mortgagee will be paid out of the other property and the property remains as a thing dedicated.

But if the dedicator has no other property, then the dedicated thing is sold, and the mortgagee is paid.

A property may be dedicated although occupied.

ART. 62.—It is not an indispensable condition that the dedicated thing should not be occupied.

Therefore the dedication of a property occupied by a thing belonging to the dedicator or a third person is valid.

E.g. If some one dedicates a house in which there are things belonging to himself or a stranger without clearing it, the dedication is valid.

The thing dedicated must be the property of the dedicator when dedicated.

ART. 63.—It is necessary that the thing dedicated should be the property of the dedicator at the time of the dedication.

Therefore an arbitrary dedication of a thing belonging to another person, made without the authority of the owner is not valid.

Unless owner ratifies.

But if, after the thing has been so dedicated, the owner approves of the dedication, the dedication becomes valid (*see note*).

Subsequent ownership not sufficient.

A thing is not considered as vaqf if some one has dedicated it arbitrarily without the approval of the owner, even if the dedicator subsequently become the owner of it.

E.g. If some one has arbitrarily dedicated a thing belonging to a relation of his, who subsequently dies without approving the dedication, the inheritance belongs exclusively to the person who has arbitrarily dedicated the thing.

Or, if a man has wrongfully appropriated a thing and dedicated it and afterwards buys it from the person who suffered from the wrongful appropriation, the thing so dedicated without the authority of the owner is not looked upon as dedicated by reason of the unauthorised dedication.

Also, if a person, who holds vaqf property by Ijaretein, dedicate it in favour of some philanthropic establishment, the dedication is invalid (*see note*). *Ijaretein vaqf cannot be dedicated.*

In the same way if the heirs of a deceased person, whose debts exceed the property left by him, dedicate to some establishment immovable property, forming part of the estate, without making themselves owners of it by releasing it and paying its value to the creditors, the dedication is not valid. *Heirs cannot dedicate when debts exceed estate.*

For which reason the creditors not consenting to the dedication made in the way described, are entitled to include the property in the division to be made (*see notes*). *Unless creditors consent.*

ART. 64.—The thing dedicated is not required to be a thing separated. *An undivided share may be dedicated.*

For which reason the fact that a share dedicated is undivided either originally or by virtue of facts subsequently ascertained, does not invalidate the dedication.

E.g. If one dedicates an undivided share in a property such as a half or a quarter, the dedication is valid whether the property is capable of division or not.

Also if, after a person has dedicated the whole of a property as his, another person comes forward and claims and recovers an undivided share as his, such as a half or a third of that estate, and after it has been decided on proof and oath that this share belongs to him, the dedication of the rest of the estate, after the deduction of the said share, being valid, is not rescinded.

But the dedication of an undivided part of a property for the purpose of its being turned into a Mesjid or cemetery is not valid whether the thing is capable of division or not. *Except for a Mesjid or cemetery.*

ART. 65.—The thing dedicated must be a defined and known thing. *The thing dedicated must be defined and known.*

Consequently, the dedication is not valid if one says, indefinitely, that he dedicates something out of his estate, or one of two workshops, or ten olive trees, indefinitely, out of those he has in his olive grove, or, indefinitely, so many pics out of his building site.

But the dedication is valid if one dedicates the undivided share in an estate of which he is part owner with another, without defining the quantity of his undivided share.

Not necessary to declare the boundaries. ART. 66.—In order that a dedication may be valid, it is not required that the boundaries of the dedicated property should be declared.

Consequently, the dedication of a property, which happens to be known by a mark or by description, is valid although the boundaries are not declared.

The dedication. ART. 67.—It is necessary that the dedication should be complete.

Must not depend on an uncertain condition. Whence a dedication is not valid which depends on something which is uncertain and does not exist at the time of dedication.

E.g. If one says " let such a thing of mine be dedicated, if my son, who is in another town comes," or " if I recover from the illness into which I have fallen," and, subsequently, if, in the first case, the son comes from that city, and in the second case, he recovers from his illness, the dedication is not valid.

ART. 68.—When a dedication depends on a thing which exists and is certain, it is considered complete.

Consequently a dedication dependent on a thing which exists and is certain at the time of the dedication is valid.

E.g. If one showing a thing of which he is owner say : " let this be dedicated if it is my property," the dedication is valid.

Dedication must not take effect in the future. Again a dedication is not valid which is referred to future time.

E.g. If one say that he dedicates some property of his from a future time, the dedication is not valid, although that time elapse.

In the same way, if one say " let such a property of mine be dedicated after my death," the property is not forthwith vaqf.

Dedication to take effect on death looked on as a bequest, *see* Art. 86. But since, in such a case, the dedication of that property is looked upon as a bequest, if this person die persisting in such a bequest, the whole of that estate is considered, as validly dedicated, if it does not exceed a third of his estate, or the heirs assent to it.

About this point, mention will be made in full in Section I, Chapter II.

Dedication invalid if option reserved. ART. 69.—In dedication there must be no condition giving the dedicator an option.

Consequently, a dedication made with an option reserved is invalid.

E.g. If one dedicates something having the option to invalidate or complete the dedication within a time, the dedication is in general invalid, whether that time is known or unknown.

But if the dedicator, having the option, dedicate the property that it may become a Mesjid, the dedication is valid and the option invalid.

Where Mesjid dedicated option invalid.

ART. 70.—The dedication must be perpetual, consequently a temporary dedication is invalid.

Temporary dedication is invalid.

E.g. Dedication is not valid, if one dedicates his estate upon the condition that it should be dedicated property for ten years, and after that return to his ownership.

Again dedication is not valid if the dedicator impose a condition opposed to the perpetual existence of the dedicated property.

E.g. Dedication is not valid if any one dedicating his immovable property put as a condition that he can, in case of need, sell it and spend the price for his own purposes.

But if he put as a condition, that the dedicated property may be sold in the future, and other more beneficial property bought for the vaqf with the price thereof, in such a case the dedication is valid and the condition is of force.

A power to sell and buy other property is good, see Art. 90.

Nevertheless the approval of the judge must be obtained when the property is to be sold under the said condition.

ART. 71.—The thing in favour of which the dedication is made must be finally determined.

The beneficiary must not be doubtful, see Art. 75.

Consequently, a dedication is invalid if the beneficiary is doubtful or ambiguous.

E.g. If any one dedicating his property say that he dedicates the thing to such a place of worship or such a school, without fixing finally the one of the two, but doubtfully and ambiguously, the dedication is invalid.

The validity of the dedication is not prejudiced if the option is left to the Mutevelli to spend the produce of the thing dedicated between certain establishments.

Option may be left to Mutevelli.

E.g. The dedication is valid if the dedicator insert a term that the Mutevelli of the vaqf may spend the income from it, if he wish, for the requirements of such a school, or, if he wish, for the needs of such a hospital.

The dedication is valid, if the dedicator put as a condition that the Mutevelli may spend the profits for the benefit of a subject which he considers as a philanthropic object.

ART. 72.—Buildings and trees which it is proposed to dedicate must not be liable to be pulled down.

Buildings and trees liable to be pulled down cannot be dedicated.

Consequently, the dedication of a building or tree liable to be pulled down is invalid.

E.g. If one make a building for himself on land which he has wrongfully appropriated and afterwards dedicate that building for the benefit of some establishment, the dedication is void.

Again, if one erect buildings or plant trees without the leave of the land authorities on Arazi mirié land, which he possesses by Tapou, and afterwards dedicates the buildings or trees, the dedication is void (Land Code, Sec. 35).

See Sec. 85.

In the same way, if one raise buildings or plant trees for himself, without the leave of the Mutevelli, on a vaqf site, which he possesses by rent, and afterwards dedicate the buildings or trees for the benefit of some establishment, the dedication is not valid (Mejellé, Art. 906).

But the dedication is valid if the building has been erected or the trees planted with the consent of the land authorities or, in the case of vaqf land, with the consent of the Mutevelli (Land Law, Sec. 25).

ART. 73.—If one plants trees on Arazi mirié which he holds by Tapou, without the permission of the land authorities and three years have elapsed and the trees have so far developed that he enjoys the fruit of them, they can be validly dedicated (Land Law, Sec. 25).

The object of the dedication must be a subject of reverence.

ART. 74.—The object in favour of which the dedication is made must be, in itself and in the conscience of the dedicator, of a kind that is the subject of reverence and worship.

Consequently, a dedication for the advancement of an object, which is neither in itself nor in the conscience of the dedicator, an object of reverence and worship, is invalid.

Again, a dedication is not valid if it is for the advancement of an object, which is in itself an object of reverence and worship, but not in the conscience of the dedicator, or which is, in the conscience of the dedicator an object of reverence and worship, but not in itself.

Beneficiary need not be declared and fixed.

ART. 75.—It is not required that the object for the benefit of which the dedication is made should be declared and fixed.

Consequently, the dedication of a thing is valid even if the object for the benefit of which it is made is not declared.

In such a case the income from the dedicated property is spent absolutely for the benefit of the poor.

Beneficiary may be a class of persons generally.

ART. 76.—It is not required that the object for which the dedication is made should be fixed and limited.

E.g. A dedication of a property in order that the income may go to the poor in general is good.

Beneficiary may be nonexistent at time of dedication.

ART. 77.—It is not required that the object for the benefit of which the dedication is made should exist at the time of the dedication.

THE LAWS OF EVQAF. 15

E.g. The dedication is valid if one who has no children dedicate his estate limiting the income for the benefit of his children.

In such a case, the children of the dedicator born after the dedication have a right to the income by virtue of the limitation.

Also the dedication is valid, if one has prepared a place for the erection of a philanthropic establishment such as a temple or school, and before the establishment is built, dedicates some of his properties for its benefit and limits the income for its advancement. After the establishment is raised, the income of the dedicated property belongs to it.

Until the birth of the child in the first case and until the erection of the building in the second case, the income is spent for the benefit of the poor.

Such a dedication in which the object of the trust did not exist at the beginning is called " Munqati'-el-evvel."

ART. 78.—If the object for the benefit of which the dedication is made exists at the beginning, but afterwards is wanting and is discontinued, it is called " Munqati'-el-akhir."

E.g. If the dedicator limit the income of the dedicated property to the benefit of his descendants, and after the descendants have enjoyed the income for some time they become extinct, the dedication is called " Munqati'-el-akhir."

ART. 79.—If the beneficiary under the dedication exist at the beginning, ceases for a time and afterwards comes into existence again, the dedication is called " Munqati'-el-wasat."

E.g. If the dedicator has limited the income of the dedicated property to the benefit of the males of his descendants and after the males have enjoyed the fruit for a time they die leaving daughters only, and after a time male children are born of the daughters, such a dedication is called " Munqati'-el-wasat."

In all sorts of vacant vaqfs where there is no existing beneficiary, the income appointed for the beneficiary is spent on the poor.

ART. 80.—If the beneficiary, in whose favour a dedication is made is likely to fail, the dedicator ought to declare and add some lasting object.

E.g. When one dedicates the income of a vaqf to the poor of his descendants, he ought to declare and add also some lasting object, saying : " If my descendants fail and this limitation becomes incapable of execution, let the income of the dedicated property be applied for the benefit of the poor."

SECTION III.

Valid and invalid dedications.

Dedication of purchase before and after price paid.

ART. 81.—If anyone dedicate a thing which he has bought from someone else before it is received, the following rules are observed :

If he dedicate it after the payment of the price to the seller, the dedication is valid.

If he dedicate it before the payment of the price, the dedication is dependent. When he pays the price, the dedication becomes valid and final.

Dedication of purchase by defective sale before and after receipt.

ART. 82.—The purchaser can dedicate a thing which he has purchased by a defective sale after its receipt.

After such a dedication, the vendor has no longer the right to rescind the sale.

The dedicator, however, must indemnify the vendor for the value of the thing dedicated.

But the buyer cannot, before receipt, dedicate a thing which he has purchased by a defective sale.

A defective gift is looked upon with reference to this subject as a defective sale (Mejellé, Arts. 109, 371-373).

A thing bought by an invalid sale cannot be dedicated.

ART. 83.—The dedication of a thing bought by an invalid sale is invalid, even if the purchaser dedicate it after delivery.

E.g. If one has bought the property of an orphan from the trustee for a price excessively below its valuation and afterwards dedicate it to some object, the dedication is invalid.

Consequently, when the infant becomes of age he takes back that property from the Mutevelli of the charity in possession.

Also if he buys a thing dedicated by irrevocable dedication and dedicates it again to some object, the second dedication is void.

In the same way, if someone has bought an estate belonging to the Beit-ul-mal for a sum excessively below its equivalent value and dedicate it to some object, the dedication is invalid.

Dedication of a thing bought or sold, with an option to rescind.

ART. 84.—If one buy and receive a thing on the condition that he is to have an option to rescind the contract within a fixed time and dedicates it before the term has elapsed, the dedication is valid and the option is of no force.

Again, if one sell something under the condition that he is to have an option to rescind within a fixed time, and dedicates the thing before that time expires, the sale is of no effect and the dedication is valid.

Buildings on Vaqf site, see Art. 72.

ART. 85.—If one build, with the permission of the Mutevelli, on a vaqf site dedicated to the support of some object and afterwards dedicate the building to another object, the dedication is valid.

But if one, being the owner of a property, of which both the site and the building are Mulk, dedicate the building alone to some object, retaining his ownership in the site, the dedication is not valid.

Trees and vines, in reference to this matter, are considered as buildings.

ART. 86.—If one dedicate a property of his, upon the condition that he shall himself possess it for life as he wishes, and that after his death the property shall be sold and the purchase money expended on philanthropic objects, the dedication is not valid.

Dedication of property to be sold subject to life interest, see Art. 68.

But as in this dedication it is considered that he makes a will that the property is to be sold and the price expended for the benefit of the poor, the rules about wills are conformed with.

ART. 87.—The person who dedicates something which he has by will left to another is considered as revoking the will.

Revocation of will by dedication.

Consequently the dedication is valid and the will of no force.

E.g. If one, after he has left by will his mulk house, dedicate it to a philanthropic object and the dedication is decided to be irrevocable, the dedication is valid and the will invalid.

In such a case, when the dedicator dies, the person in whose favour the will is made cannot contend that he is entitled to take the house by virtue of the will, on the ground that the dedicator, before the dedication, had willed the house to him and that the third of his property is sufficient for the bequest.

ART. 88.—Dedication by writing alone is not valid.
It must be made known and attested.

Writing alone not a sufficient dedication.

Consequently, if one write and compose a document of dedication for the establishment of some vaqf, but does not read that document before witnesses and make known the contents, himself calling upon them to attest it, the dedication is not valid.

ART. 89.—The fact that the dedicator limits the benefit of the dedicated thing in favour of himself or his children does not prejudice the validity of the dedication.

Dedication in favour of self or children valid.

E.g. If one dedicate a house and limit the income to be derived from it, or the right of occupying it, in favour of himself, while he lives, and in favour of his children or posterity after his death, the dedication is valid and the limitation of force.

D

Again, if one dedicates his property and direct that his debt which shall arise in the future shall be paid out of the income of the dedicated thing, the dedication is valid and the direction of force.

Dedication with power of exchange, is valid *see* Art. 70.

ART. 90.—A dedication made with a power of exchange is valid.

E.g. If one dedicate an inn which he holds as mulk and make it a term of the dedication that that inn may afterwards in case of need be exchanged for other property, the dedication is valid.

But if the dedicator insert a term in the dedication that the property which he dedicates may afterwards be sold and the price given as alms to the poor, the dedication under this condition is not valid.

Dedication of water and water rights.

ART. 91.—The dedication of the right of taking water as attached to the land and the dedication of water as attached to the water channels is valid.

Place of worship.

ART. 92.—If a man build a place in his house in order that it may be used as a Mesjid, but does not separate it and open a road that the people may come in from outside, the place is not considered as a Mesjid.

Consequently, that place is looked upon as a dependency of the house and may be possessed by the different sorts of ownership.

Place of worship.

ART. 93.—It is allowed to build a Mesjid on the upper story and to construct buildings in the lower story for the needs of the Mesjid and to dedicate them.

But it is not allowed to pull down a Mesjid built on the lower story and erect buildings in its place and a Mesjid above it.

SECTION IV.

Things which are included in a dedication without being mentioned (Mejellé, Arts. 230, 236).

Dedication of property includes rights attached to it.

ART. 94.—If one dedicates a property and does not record that he dedicates also the rights attached to it, such as the private way of the property, the right of taking water and of outflow, these rights, as attached to that property, are included in the dedication also.

Building site includes buildings, trees and vines.

ART. 95.—When a building site is dedicated, there is included in the dedication, without being mentioned, the buildings, trees and vines which are on it at the time of the dedication.

Not fruit appearing at time of dedication.

ART. 96.—The fruit, which at the time of the dedication appears on the tree is not included in the dedication, but remains the property of the dedicator. Consequently, when a vegetable plantation is made vaqf, the vegetables found therein are not included in the dedication, but remain the property of the dedicator.

ART. 97.—If a property is dedicated, and its bounds and the things which go with it are declared, and at the time of the dedication the said things are imperfectly declared, all the things which go with the property and exist within the boundaries, are considered as included in the dedication, because according to the Sacred Law the boundaries are considered. *If boundaries are declared, all things included in them are dedicated, imperfect declaration.*

E.g. If when a hotel containing 24 rooms is dedicated and it is described as containing 15 rooms and its boundaries are recorded, there is included in the dedication also the 24 rooms exactly found within the recorded boundaries.

But if, after the boundaries are recorded, he dedicate the property, excepting from the dedication certain things which go with the property, and retaining them in his ownership, in such a case the things which he has excepted are not included in the dedication. *Unless there is an express exception.*

E.g. When one declares the boundaries of a house containing men's apartments and women's apartments and wishes to dedicate it, if he keeps the ownership of the men's apartments and says that he dedicates only the women's apartments, the men's apartments are considered to be excluded from the dedication.

ART. 98.—If, after a person has made a declaration as to a fixed share in a property, which he owns jointly with another, and has dedicated it defining the amount of his share, it is shewn that his undivided share is greater than he declared, the dedication is valid and the excess is included in it. *Dedication of owner's share, false description.*

E.g. If after a man has declared that his share in a common property is composed of one-fourth and dedicated it, it is shewn that a share in that estate up to half belongs to him, the dedication is valid and the surplus is included in it.

SECTION V.

Dedications made by persons who are ill.

ART. 99.—The exercise of authority made by a debtor at a time of mortal sickness and which deprives his creditors of their rights, is not to be carried out. *Dedication by debtor in time of mortal sickness.*

Consequently, if some one, whose debts are in excess of his property, at a time of mortal sickness dedicate some of his property and die, the creditors can refuse assent to the dedication and include the dedicated thing in the division (Mejellé, Art. 800).

ART. 100.—The benefactions made by a person who has no heirs, at a time of mortal sickness, are valid up to the whole of his property. *Benefactions by person who has no heirs—in time of mortal sickness valid.*

D2

Consequently, if one who has no heirs dedicate the whole of his property, at a time of mortal sickness to some object of common benefit, the dedication is valid and must be carried out.

In such a case, after the death of the benefactor, the director of the Beit-ul-mal cannot interfere with the property (Mejellé, Art. 877).

Where there are heirs, valid to one-third of estate only, unless, heirs approve. ART. 101.—The benefactions, made at a time of mortal sickness by one who has heirs, are of force up to one-third only of his estate, unless the heirs approve of the portion given in excess of a third.

Consequently, if some one, at the time of his illness of which he dies, dedicate something, and the dedication is decided to be irrevocable and after this the dedicator die, the following rules are observed :—

If the third of his estate is not less than the property dedicated, the dedication is valid in every case whether the heirs approve of it or not.

If the third of his estate is less than the property dedicated, the whole of that property is considered as dedicated if the heirs approve of it. If the heirs do not approve, the third of the property becomes vaqf and the heirs take the rest of the inheritance. If some of the heirs approve and some do not, in addition to the third of the estate, the shares of the heirs who approve constitute part of the dedication.

In such a case, if after an heir who disapproves has taken his share from the dedicated property and sold it to another, other property of the dedicator is found and it is proved that the third of his estate is not less than the dedicated property, the sale is not dissolved and remains in force.

But that heir makes indemnity for the portion sold. And for the amount received by way of indemnity another thing is bought, in order that it may be dedicated in substitution for the portion sold (Mejellé, Art. 879).

Consent of heirs must be given after death of dedicator. ART. 102.—The consent of the heirs with regard to the amount in excess of one-third must be given after the death of the dedicator.

Consequently, the consent or refusal of the heirs before the death of the dedicator is not taken into consideration.

Assent of heir does not apply to property inherited from dissenting heir. ART. 103.—When some one, after he has dedicated some property of his, during the illness of which he dies, leaves two heirs, and the third of the property of the deceased is less than the thing dedicated, and one of the heirs assents to the dedication of the property in excess of the third of the estate, and the other heir dies, not having assented to it, even if the estate of the latter pass to the heir who previously assented, it is none the less required that he, who accepted the validity of the dedication, should assent again to the validity of the dedication of the excess of the third of the estate, as regards the share of the deceased heir, the former assent is not sufficient.

ART. 104.—If any one, having no heir except his wife dedicate, while in his last illness, the whole of his estate and die after the dedication has been decided to be irrevocable, all the estate of the deceased becomes vaqf if the wife assents to the dedication. *When dedicator, in mortal sickness, has no heirs but wife.*

But if the wife do not consent, the sixth of the inheritance belongs to the wife and the remainder becomes vaqf.

ART. 105.—If a woman, having no heir, except her husband, dedicate the whole of her estate, and after the act of dedication has been decided to be irrevocable die, all the estate of the deceased is constituted a vaqf if the husband assent to the act of dedication. *Or, no heir but husband.*

If the husband do not consent, the third of the inheritance is given to him and the remainder is looked upon as vaqf.

ART. 106.—A state of sickness which is cured is looked upon as a state of health. *Sickness from which dedicator recovers.*

Consequently, if one, being sick and confined to his bed, dedicate some of his property, and the dedication is decided to be irrevocable, and afterwards the sick person recover from his sickness, and after he has been well for some time, die, his heirs cannot refuse to agree to the dedication, in so far as it exceeds the third of his estate, on the ground that the dedicator made the dedication while he was ill (Mejellé, Art. 595).

ART. 107.—A person who has a protracted illness extending over more than a year is considered as a person in health, so long as his condition does not change. *Protracted illness.*

Consequently, if one, who is fallen into protracted illness lasting more than a year, dedicate some of his property, and the dedication is judicially decided to be irrevocable without his condition being changed, and after the lapse of some days, his condition is changed, and the illness becomes bad and he dies, the dedication is of force for the whole estate of the deceased.

In such a case the heirs of the deceased cannot contend that they do not accept the dedication, so far as relates to the excess over a third of his estate.

But if the person proceeds to the dedication after his condition is changed, then that dedication is valid up to the third.

Consequently the heirs can refuse their assent to the dedication of the part of the estate in excess of one-third.

Dedication in
favour of an
heir, with or
without limi-
tation over.

ART. 108.—If a person, at the time of his fatal illness, dedicate something of his, limiting its benefit in favour of one of his heirs, and, after the death of the heir, to some philanthropic object, and afterwards die, that dedication is valid if a third of the estate is not less than the thing dedicated.

In such a case if the other heirs assent to the act of dedication, the heir in whose favour the limitation is made enjoys the benefit of the dedicated property alone.

If the other heirs do not assent, the heir in whose favour the benefit is limited, does not enjoy the benefit of the dedicated property alone, but while he lives the other heirs enjoy the benefit with him, according to the share to which they are entitled by inheritance.

If while the heir, in whose favour the dedication is made, is alive, one of the other heirs die, the heirs of the deceased stand in his place as regards the right to enjoy the benefit.

If the heir, in whose favour the act of dedication is made dies, the benefit of the thing dedicated belongs entirely to the philanthropic object to which it was limited on the death of the heir. No right remains any more to the other heirs to benefit from it.

But if one, in his last sickness, dedicate something of his, limiting its benefit in favour of some of his heirs and do not declare another philanthropic object, in such a case, when the other heirs do not assent to the act of dedication, it is invalid, although the third of the estate is not less than it, and all the heirs inherit the thing.

Dedication for
place of
worship.

ART. 109.—If someone dedicate, at the time of his last illness, an estate of his in order that a Mesjid may be built and die, and the third of his estate is less than the thing dedicated, the dedication of the whole of that property is invalid if the heirs do not assent to the dedication of the part exceeding one-third the value of the estate.

Consequently the heirs inherit that estate altogether.

Dedication in
health and
judicial sanc-
tion during
mortal illness.

ART. 110.—If the act of dedication is made in a state of sound health, and is judicially declared irrevocable when the dedicator is in a state of mortal sickness, the condition at the time of the dedication and not that at the time of the judicial decision governs the matter.

Consequently, if one dedicates his estate, at a time when he is in health, without a judicial decision of the irrevocability of the act of dedication, and after this at the time of his mortal sickness, causes the dedication to be judicially declared irrevocable and dies, that dedication is valid for the whole of his estate and not up to the third of it.

Consequently, in such a case, the heirs of the dedicator cannot contend that, since the judicial decision took place at the time of mortal sickness, the dedication is valid to the third of the estate and not to an amount exceeding one-third.

CHAPTER II.

Irrevocable and revocable acts of dedication.

SECTION I.

Irrevocable acts of dedication.

ART. 111.—After the completion of the dedication, its irrevocability depends on the formalities described below :— **Dedication irrevocable.**

The first formality consists in the decision of a judge in favour of its irrevocability after trial. **After judicial decision that it is so.**

Thus if someone, after he has dedicated, in the manner prescribed by Section II. Chapter I., some specific thing of which he is the owner, and given it to the Mutevelli appointed by him to have it declared irrevocable by the Court, wishes to recall the act of dedication, and to take back from the Mutevelli that thing, in order that it may be his own property as before, but the Mutevelli does not agree to the giving back of the thing, and so, when a dispute and difference of opinion has sprung up between the dedicator and the Mutevelli, if the case is tried before some judge having knowledge of the different opinions of the mujtehids about the irrevocability or otherwise of a dedication, and the judge decides in favour of the irrevocability of the dedication according to the opinion of a mujtehid allowing the validity of the dedication, in such a case the dedication is irrevocable.

If without such trial being gone through, the judge in compliance merely with the demand of the dedicator or the Mutevelli, decide in favour of the irrevocability of the act of dedication, its irrevocability does not result from the judge having so said (*see note*).

ART. 112.—By the decision of an arbitrator the act of dedication is not rendered irrevocable. **Decision of arbitrator not sufficient.**

Thus if the dedicator and the Mutevelli appointed by him to have the dedication judicially declared irrevocable, appoint an arbitrator, and he decides in favour of its irrevocability, the dedication is not established as irrevocable.

The dedication is made irrevocable by the decision of a judge appointed by the Sultan.

When the dedicator dies before the judicial decision of the irrevocability of the dedication and the heirs demand before the judge from the Mutevelli that they may include the dedicated thing in the inheritance and divide it, but **Judicial decision after death of dedicator.**

the Mutevelli refuses to give it up, the dedication is decided to be irrevocable if the judge decide in favour of the irrevocability of the dedication and restrain the heirs from annoying the Mutevelli.

Again, when one, having no debts and being in health, dedicate some things of his, without a judicial decision in favour of the dedication, and, after the lapse of some time, dies, leaving debts greater than his estate, and the creditors bring an action against the Mutevelli before the judge, seeking to include the dedicated things in the division for the body of the creditors, and the Mutevelli refuses to give it up, a judicial decision of the irrevocability of the dedication is considered as having been made if the judge decide in favour of the irrevocability of the dedication and restrain the creditors from annoying the Mutevelli.

Irrevocable, if made by will, up to the amount disposable.

ART. 113.—The second formality consists in the establishment of the dedication by will.

Thus if one make a will saying " when I die, let such a thing of mine be dedicated to such a philanthropic object " and afterwards dies without changing his will that thing becomes vaqf by irrevocable dedication, if the third of his estate is not less than the property so left.

But if the third of the estate is less than the property willed, in such a case only a sum equal to one-third of his estate becomes vaqf by irrevocable dedication. The part in excess of that amount is inherited by the heirs.

But if the heirs assent to the will as regards the surplus over the third, in such a case the whole sum bequeathed becomes vaqf by an irrevocable act of dedication.

In the case in which the person so making a will has no heir, there also the whole thing bequeathed becomes vaqf by an irrevocable act of dedication.

Arts. 101, 103, 104 and 105 are applicable as regards this matter.

Dedication not irrevocable unless there is judicial decision, or it is made by will.

ART. 114.—If neither of the above mentioned two forms exist, the dedication is not made irrevocable.

There are excepted however the two cases below, for the irrevocability of the dedication of which neither of the two above mentioned formalities is required.

Exception, place of worship.

(a). If one separate from his property a Mesjid with the building and a way to it, and give leave to the people to worship in it and the people assemble there and worship aloud, that Mesjid becomes vaqf by an irrevocable dedication.

Exception, cemetery.

(b). If one having dedicated his building site to be used as a cemetery, give permission to bury the dead there, and a dead person is buried in it, that building site becomes vaqf by irrevocable dedication.

ART. 115.—The fact that dedicated property is added to property formerly dedicated does not make the dedication irrevocable.

Additions to dedicated property are not *ipso facto* irrevocable dedications, *compare* Art. 123.

Thus when one dedicates some of his property, and the dedication is judicially declared irrevocable, and afterwards he dedicates certain other of his properties without the dedication being judicially declared irrevocable, saying that he adds these last properties to those dedicated by him at first through the judicial declaration of the validity of the act dedicating those properties, merely by his saying so, the things subsequently dedicated are not made vaqf by irrevocable dedication.

In order that they should be made irrevocably vaqf, there is required another special decision of the Court in favour of their irrevocability.

Special decision of judge required.

ART. 116.—If one dedicates his property to one object, but before he deliver it to the Muteveli and the dedication is decided to be irrevocable in accordance with the Sacred Law, he recall the dedication and dedicate the property to another object and gets a judicial decision of the irrevocability of the dedication to be made, the first act of dedication is invalid and the second act of dedication valid and irrevocable.

Revocation before decision of judge.

ART. 117.—It is forbidden to the judges by Imperial Order to pronounce irrevocable the dedications of debtors.

Dedication of debtor's property not valid, although judicial sanction given.

Consequently if a debtor, even if he continues in good health, dedicate his property and afterwards die, not leaving sufficient other property to pay his debt, the creditors can annul the dedication on application to the judge and receive their claims from that property.

In such a case if the judge does not annul the dedication and decides in favour of its irrevocability and validity, neither is the judgment to be executed nor is the decision of the Court in favour of the irrevocability of the dedication of any force (*see* Irade A.H. 950).

But if someone, at a time when he does not owe anything and continues in good health, dedicate properties of his and obtain the judicial sanction, and afterwards the dedicator dies in debt, leaving no estate, his creditors cannot interfere with the dedicated properties (*see* Cyprus Law, VII. of 1886).

ART. 118.—It is forbidden to the judges to declare in favour of the validity of an act dedicating a ghedik.

Dedication of ghedic not valid.

For which reason when one dedicates ghedik, which he possesses, if the judge decides in favour of the irrevocability of the dedication and confirms it, neither is his decision nor the confirmation of force (*see* Irade 18 Zilhijje, 1277).

SECTION II.

Rules and questions relating to the irrevocability or otherwise of the act of dedication.

Dedicator cannot deal with dedicated property.

ART. 119.—If one dedicates a thing by an irrevocable act of dedication, he cannot any more have the ownership of it and exercise dominion over it.

Every act of dominion over it is invalid.

E.g. If one sell, or give, or pledge a thing which he has dedicated by an irrevocable dedication, these agreements are invalid.

Again a thing dedicated by irrevocable dedication does not pass by inheritance to the heirs.

Dedicated thing given in exchange treated as mulk.

But if the thing dedicated by an irrevocable dedication is exchanged, in conformity with the rules laid down in a special chapter, for another thing, the thing taken in exchange becomes vaqf in the place of the thing first dedicated and the latter reverts into mulk property and is governed by the laws concerning it.

Where person with right of pre-emption recovers.

Again when it is shewn that a third person has a legal right of pre-emption over a property, which someone has bought from another, even if the purchaser has dedicated that property and obtained a judicial decision of the irrevocability of the dedication, the act of dedication is annulled on the demand and action of the person having the right of pre-emption, and that property is given as pure mulk to the person who has the right of pre-emption.

Materials of building destroyed.

Likewise, if the building of a roofed property dedicated by irrevocable dedication is destroyed entirely, and, the vaqf not being rich, it is impossible to rebuild the property and to use the material remaining for building, the Mutevelli is allowed to sell that material at its equivalent value for the good of the dedication.

Dead trees in garden.

Again the Mutevelli of a garden dedicated by an irrevocable dedication may root out dead trees and sell them at the equivalent value for the good of the dedication.

Stranger proving claim to property.

ART. 120.—If after someone has dedicated a thing which he has bought from another and the dedication has been judicially declared irrevocable, someone appears who claims it, and brings an action claiming that the thing dedicated is his property and prove his contention according to the Sacred Law, and the thing is adjudged to be the property of the claimant, after he has taken an oath, the dedication is annulled and the claimant takes that thing.

In such a case the buyer can bring an action and recover from the seller the price received, and become owner of it, with no obligation to buy another thing for that price and dedicate it, in the place of the thing which has been recovered and taken from him.

ART. 121.—The dedication of a thing, not irrevocably **Revocation by judge.** dedicated, when dissolved by the judge, is of no force. The thing is possessed as mulk.

E.g. If a person dedicate his workshop which he owns as mulk, but before he hands it over to the Mutevelli and gets a decision in favour of the dedication according to the Sheri' Law, he becomes insolvent and in misfortune in such a way, that, being compelled to deal with that workshop as his mulk property, he wishes to recall the dedication, he applies at first to the judge to dissolve the dedication.

When the judge dissolves the dedication, the dedicator possesses the thing dedicated as his mulk property.

The same thing also happens if the heirs of the dedicator dissolve the dedication through the medium of the judge.

If a thing, which is not irrevocably dedicated be sold to another, without its dedication having been dissolved by the judge, and the judge after trial decide in favour of the validity of the sale, the dedication is not valid (Mejellé, 864).

ART. 122.—If one dedicates property of his by a will, **Revocation by revocation of will.** on the condition that it is to be in force as a dedication after his death, that thing is not taken from the ownership of the dedicator before he dies, without revoking the will.

Consequently, the dedicator possesses that thing as his pure mulk as long as he lives, being able even at the time of his mortal sickness to recall that will of his by words and acts.

The person, who revokes a will by words, must use words **Of will by words.** declaring the revocation of his will, such as " I revoke my will " or " I give it up."

The person, who revokes his will by act, must exercise **By act.** his power over the thing which he dedicated in such a way as to change the name of the thing, or extinguish his ownership in it.

E.g. If anyone has made a bequest by the words " let such a mulk building site of mine be dedicated after my death, and afterwards build on that site a house or workshop or plant in it vines and trees and change the building site into a vineyard or garden, or put an end to his ownership in it by sale, or gift and delivery, since thus, by act, he has revoked the bequest, it is no longer of force.

For the making of such a revocation, an application to the judge is not required.

ART. 123.—The revocation of a thing done for the **Expenditure incurred for a dedication cannot be recoverd.** benefit of a vaqf has no force. **compare Art. 115.**

E.g. A man cannot, after he has built on a dedicated building site at his own expense and given the building for the benefit of the vaqf, revoke the gift and take the building as his own private property.

Again, after a person has given a sum of money to the Mutevelli to spend for the affairs of the vaqf and the Mutevelli has spent and laid out the money for those affairs he cannot revoke the gift and seek indemnification from the Mutevelli for this sum.

CHAPTER III.
Lands dedicated.

Dedicated lands of two sorts.
ART. 124.—Dedicated lands are of two sorts :—
(a). Dedicated lands which belong to true (sahiha) vaqfs.

True dedicated lands and Takhsisat.
(b). Lands which do not belong to true vaqfs.
That is to say dedicated lands which belong to the category of Takhsisat (Land Law, Sec. 4).

True dedicated land Ushrie and Kharajié.
ART. 125.—Arazi ushrie and Arazi kharajié dedicated in the manner provided by the Sacred Law, by the owner, are true vaqfs, (Land Law, Sec. 2).

Mevat acquired as mulk.
ART. 126.—If one cultivate mevat land, with the leave of the Sultan, in order that he may make it his own mulk property and afterwards dedicate that land to some philanthropic object, such a vaqf is a true vaqf (Mejellé, Arts. 1270, 1280).

Arazi mirié acquired as mulk.
ART. 127.—If a piece of Arazi mirié is given by the Imperial Government into the ownership of some one as his mulk and this person dedicates that piece to some philanthropic object, such a vaqf is true vaqf.

Arazi mirié must be acquired by purchase.
ART. 128.—In order that a grant of land as mulk may be valid, the person obtaining the grant must acquire it by a valid purchase.

Thus when the mulk ownership of Arazi mirié is granted by the Imperial Government, the following things are required from the person who seeks it :

If when the mulk ownership is granted, the Beit-ul-mal is pressed by want, in order that the grant may be valid, the person who acquires the mulk ownership must buy the land from the Beit-ul-mal for its equivalent value and pay the sum.

In such a case, if it was purchased for a price excessively below the value, the mulk ownership is not validly granted.

But if at the time of the grant of the mulk ownership the Beit-ul-mal is not pressed by want, then the person who acquires the mulk ownership must purchase the piece of land for double the value.

In such a case, if it is purchased for a price excessively below the double of its value, the mulk ownership is not validly granted.

ART. 129.—The grant of the mulk ownership of Arazi mirié depends on the public benefit.

Sale of Arazi mirié must be for public benefit.

Consequently if the grant of the mulk ownership of Arazi mirié is injurious to the common weal, the grant is never allowed nor is it lawful.

ART. 130.—By a document of grant of ownership (temlik-name) alone, the grant is not validly completed.

Grant of Arazi mirié without sale invalid.

Thus, if one does not buy by a valid purchase (as mentioned in the preceding articles) a piece of Arazi mirié from the Beit-ul-mal, and the mulk ownership is given to him as a gift, and a document of grant given to him, such grant of ownership is not validly effected.

ART. 131.—Places dedicated, without their mulk ownership, by the Sultans out of Arazi mirié, for philanthropic objects of which the expense is borne by the Beit-ul-mal, belong to the Takhsisat category (see Arts. 128, 129 & 130).

Takhsisat lands. Public land dedicated by Sultan without ownership.

ART. 132.—If someone, without having obtained the valid mulk ownership of Arazi mirié, dedicate the land with the permission of the Sultan, in favour of philanthropic objects of which the expense is borne by the Beit-ul-mal, the vaqf is considered as one of the Takhsisat category.

Dedication of public land, of which ownership is not acquired by the Sultan's leave for public objects.

Art. 133.—If someone, without having obtained a valid mulk ownership of a field being Arazi mirié, which he possesses by Tapou, or without receiving the leave of the Sultan dedicate it in favour of some object, the thing so dedicated is not regarded as true vaqf or as a Takhsisat vaqf, but as before it is regarded as simple Arazi mirié.

Public land of which ownership is not acquired, dedicated without Sultan's leave not vaqf.

Consequently that person possesses that field in the same way as he did before and pays a tithe to the Beit-ul-mal, if he wishes to sell it to another he does so by the leave of the land authorities. After his death that field belongs to his heirs, if there are any persons entitled to inherit according to the Land Law, if there are not, it escheats to the Beit-ul-mal as being without owner and is granted for the Tapou value to the person claiming it.

The dedication made in the manner described has no force.

ART. 134.—If the tithe and the Kharaj, which belongs to the public out of the Ushrie and Kharajié lands which are under the mulk ownership of someone, is dedicated and specially assigned by His Majesty the Sultan to some object supported by the Beit-ul-mal, such a vaqf is of the Takhsisat category.

Takhsisat-Tithe and Kharaj.

ART. 135.—If it is known that a dedicator before its dedication, bought from the Beit-ul-mal a field originally Arazi mirié, but from time immemorial dedicated, that field is considered a true vaqf, whether it is known that that

Proof of public lands being dedicated knowledge of purchase.

purchase was made in conformity with the legal manner described in Art. 128 or not.

But if it is not known at all that the dedicator purchased that field from the public before the dedication, that field can no longer be considered a true vaqf.

Proof required that ownership lapsed before dedication.

ART. 136.—No consideration is given to the probability of the thing which is not based on proof.

Whence, the probability that perhaps the owner of a field which is situated in a place of which the lands pay tithe or kharaj, and which is dedicated from time immemorial, died without heirs, and that perhaps this field reverted to the ownership of the State, and to the class of Arazi mirié, and was dedicated afterwards, without a grant of ownership, does not make it possible that it should be regarded as not true vaqf, on account of the mere probability which is not based on proof.

Takhsisat dedications of public lands, three kinds.

ART. 137.—Arazi mirié, which has been made vaqf of the Takhsisat category by a dedication which is not a true (sahiha) dedication, is of three kinds :—

(*a*). Lands of which only the tithes and taxes (rusumat) have been dedicated and consecrated by the Government, while the right of possession (huquq tasarruf) over them, as well as the ownership (raqabe) belong as before to the Beit-ul-mal.

(*b*). Lands of which the tithes and taxes belong as before to the Beit-ul-mal and only the right to their possession (huquq-i-tasarruf) has been dedicated and assigned to some object by the Government.

(*c*). Lands of which both the right of possession (huquq tasarruf) as well as the tithes and taxes have been dedicated and assigned to some object by the Government.

Right of beneficiary in first kind.

The tithes and such taxes as the tax on grant or inheritance and the price of unowned land, belong to the dedication of the first kind.

Since the rights over the lands of this sort belong to the State, they are granted as other Arazi mirié by the State for cultivation.

Right of dedication in second and third sorts.

The lands of the second and third sort are possessed by the vaqf, whether sown, cultivated or rented to others or given on an agreement to be cultivated in partnership.

But the tithes of the second sort are paid to the State. while the tithes of the third sort are not paid.

Of these three sorts, only the first is regulated by the rules of the Land Law.

Since the right of the possession of the other two sorts does not belong to the State, the rules of the Land Law are not applied to them.

ART. 138.—The special acts of dedication (Takhsis) are of two sorts :— *(marginal: Takhsisat dedications true and untrue.)*

(*a*). A true Takhsis, which consists in the special dedication of part of the income belonging to the Beit-ul-mal to some object supported by the Beit-ul-mal.

(*b*). An untrue Takhsis, which consists in the special dedication of part of the income of the Beit-ul-mal to some object not supported at the expense of the Beit-ul-mal.

The income of the first sort, being specially dedicated is spent on the object for which it is dedicated and does not admit of revocation or being made invalid. *(marginal: True Takhsisat dedication irrevocable.)*

The second sort can be revoked and made invalid at the will of the Sultan. *(marginal: Untrue revocable.)*

ART. 139.—When someone dedicates a place out of Ushrie and Kharajié lands, his tithe and kharaj is not abolished but the payment of them is due to the Beit-ul-mal, as before. *(marginal: When titheable and kharajié lands dedicated, tithe and kharaj still payable.)*

Again if, when a field is granted to someone by the Sultan out of Arazi mirié to be held as mulk, the person again dedicate that field by a deed of dedication judicially sanctioned, the lawful tithes ought to be paid as before to the Beit-ul-mal.

Consequently in one and the same subject there may co-exist both a true vaqf and an untrue vaqf of the Takhsisat sort.

Thus after some land out of the above mentioned mulk lands has been dedicated by its owner by a true dedication, if the income belonging to the Beit-ul-mal is dedicated and consecrated by the Sultan to some object, there thus co-exist in the same subject a true dedication and an untrue dedication of the Takhsisat sort.

CHAPTER IV.
Terms usually employed by dedicators.
SECTION I.
The terms of acts of dedication in favour of children, relations and neighbours.

(marginal: See also Art. 371.)

ART. 140.—By the word " children " said once only, " legitimate children " is meant. *(marginal: Children.)*

Consequently grandchildren are not included.

E.g. If the dedicator make mention of the word " children " once only, without repeating it and say " the income of the vaqf I limit in favour of my children," the vaqf is limited in favour of his legitimate children alone and not in favour of his grandchildren.

But in the case in which, in the expression of the dedicator, there is an indication that by the word " children " grandchildren are also intended, then the word " children " includes also grandchildren.

E.g. If the dedicator say that he limits the income from the dedicated property to his children, from generation to generation, grandchildren are also included and both the lawful children and posterity of the dedicator have rights over the income of the vaqf.

Children twice. ART. 141.—The word " children " repeated twice includes all generations, whether near or remote. It is not limited to the first and second generation alone.

Consequently if, while the existing issues of the first and second generations enjoy the income of the dedicated property, which was appointed by the dedicator in favour of his children and their descendants, some children of the third generation of the dedicator are born, such children participate in the income of the dedicated property together with the issue of the first and second generations.

The children, therefore, of the first and second generations cannot bar the participation of the children of the third generation on the ground that, as the dedicator made mention of the word " children " only twice, the children of the third generation are not included.

Also if the dedicator limit the occupation of a house, which he dedicated, to his children and the children of his children and when they become extinct to the Imam of a certain Mesjid, the turn of the Imam does not come before the descendants of the dedicator are entirely extinct. The Imam does not aquire a right to live in that house after the children only of the first and second generation are extinct.

Children, grandchildren and their descendants. ART. 142.—If the dedicator of a thing dedicated by him and limited to his children and the children of his children, makes use of any word indicating the order in which the generations are to take, in such a case if the first generation exists, the second does not participate in the income of the dedicated thing.

If the dedicator say that he limits the income of the dedicated property to his children, from generation to generation, and to the children of his children, if there are legitimate children of the first generation, the children of the second generation do not participate in the income of the dedicated property.

In the same way, if there are children of the second generation, those of the third do not participate.

The same rule applies by analogy to the other generations as well.

ART. 143.—In interpreting the expressions of the dedicator the words of description are to be given effect to.
If, therefore, the dedicator, by some description, designate
the persons in whose favour the dedication is made, such
description becomes the means by which the right is
acquired, and a person not designated by such a description,
does not acquire any right in the benefit so appointed.

E.g. When the dedicator limits the income of the dedicated property to his offspring, saying : " Let such of my
children and their descendants as are residing in such a
town, enjoy the income of the property I dedicate," any
children or descendants of his not residing in that town do
not acquire any right in such benefit.

Also, if he say " Let such of my children and grandchildren as are learned (Ulema) enjoy the income of the
dedicated property," then the unlearned children and
grandchildren of the dedicator do not acquire any right in
such income of the dedicated property. In the same way,
if he say : " Let my poor children and grandchildren enjoy
the income of the dedicated property," the rich children
and grandchildren of the dedicator do not acquire any
right in such income.

The same rule applies by analogy to other descriptions
as well.

ART. 144.—The wife of a rich man, although she has no
property whatever, is considered rich.

Consequently the wife of a rich man does not participate
in the income of the dedicated property, which is limited
to the poor.

In opposition to this, the husband of a rich woman who
has no property, is not considered rich.

Consequently a husband of a rich woman who has no
property, participates in the income of the dedicated
property which is appointed for the poor.

ART. 145.—When the dedicator appoints the income of
the dedicated property to his children from generation to
generation, if a child of the first generation dies, having
said in his lifetime that the share belonging to him out of
the income should be given to his children, and if afterwards,
while some children of the first generation of the dedicator are enjoying the income of the dedicated property,
one of them die leaving children, then the deceased being
regarded as living, the income of the dedication, is divided
between the deceased child of the first generation and the
other living children in equal proportions. And the share
allotted to the deceased is given to his children.

The same rule applies when another child of the first
generation dies leaving children, until the first generation
is extinct.

E

When the first generation is entirely extinct, this division is annulled and the income of the dedicated property is equally divided among the existing children of the second generation.

Children includes child.

ART. 146.—The word " children " by custom includes one child.

Consequently if the dedicator limit the income of the dedicated property to his children, while he has only one child, such child acquires a right to the whole.

Children may mean grand-children.

ART. 147.—Sometimes the word " children," metaphorically means " grandchildren."

When all the legitimate children of a woman, who has arrived at an age at which she cannot naturally conceive, die, and if such woman while only her grandchildren are living, dedicates something, saying that she limits the income thereof to her children, as it is not possible that the word " children," should have its literal meaning " legitimate children," a metaphorical meaning is given to this word and the income is considered as having been appointed in favour of the grandchildren.

Pronoun refers to nearest noun generally.

ART. 148.—In the absence of anything shewing that the pronoun refers to a preceding word, it refers to the nearest noun.

E.g. If the dedicator write, in the deed of dedication by which he dedicates some property and which is written in Arabic " The dedicator limits the office of Mutevelli to himself, and, after his death, to his son Yahia and, afterwards to his children," the pronoun " his " in the phrase " afterwards to his children," refers to Yahia and not to the preceding word " himself."

Therefore, if in such a case the dedicator and his son Yahia die and the office of Mutevelli is taken up by the children of Yahia, the children of another son of the dedicator cannot contend that they are entitled to participate in the office of Mutevelli together with Yahia's children on the ground that the pronoun in the proposition aforesaid refers to the dedicator.

If in the deed of dedication, which is written in Turkish, it is expressed that the dedicator limits the office of Mutevelli first to his son Souleiman and, after his death, to his children, the construction is the same.

Division is to be in equal shares unless the contrary is expressed.

ART. 149.—If there be no term in the deed of dedication providing for an unequal division, the implied condition is considered to be a division in equal shares.

Consequently the income of a dedicated property, which is limited generally to the children of the dedicator, is divided equally among the male and female children of the dedicator.

No greater share is given to the male children than to the female.

Unless the dedicator directs that the income is to be divided according to the right of inheritance. In such a case the income of the dedicated property is divided among the children and his male children receive twice as much as the female.

ART. 150.—If the dedicator say : " I limit the income of the property I dedicated to my male children and to the male children of my children," in this term the male children of his daughters are included.

Male children of children includes male children of females.

ART. 151.—When the word " children " is used without restriction in the phrase used by the dedicator, the children born after the dedication are also included.

Children includes children born after the dedication.

Consequently, if the dedicator say : " I limit the income of the property I dedicate, to my children," all the children existing at the time of the dedication and those born after are included in the term (see Art. 77).

But if the dedicator designate the children by the adjective " existing," or enumerate their names and fix them in this way, in such a case the children born after the dedication is made, are not included.

E.g. If the dedicator say " I limit the income of the property I dedicate to those of my children who are existing this day," or if he say, I limit the office of Mutevelli of the property I dedicate to such and such of my children, the children born after the dedication is made are not included in the terms.

On this subject, the same rule applies to the grand-children as well.

ART. 152.—The word children of children does not only mean the children of the male children but those of the female too.

Children of children includes children of female children.

Consequently, the income of the dedicated property, which is limited to the children of the dedicator's children, is divided among the children of the dedicator's son and the children of his daughter.

The particulars aforesaid are also applied to the office of Mutevelli.

ART. 153.—The legitimate children and the parents of a person are not included where the dedication is in favour of his relations.

Relations does not include children and parents.

Consequently, the legitimate children and the parents of the dedicator are not included in the dedication, the benefit of which is limited by the dedicator in favour of his relations.

ART. 154.—If a Mussulman dedicator limits the benefit of the property dedicated by him to his relations without

Relations includes Mussulman and non-Mussulman.

qualification, the non-Mussulman relations of the dedicator are included.

Also, if a non-Mussulman dedicator limit the benefit of the property dedicated by him to his relations without qualification, his Mussulman relations are also included in this term (*see* Art. 76).

But if the dedicator limits the benefit of the property dedicated to his relations who belong to the same religion, in such a case his relations, who have a different creed, are not included in the term (*see* Art. 143).

Power given to guardian. ART. 155.—When a man, after he has made a will that the third of his property is to be dedicated, after his death, to some philanthropic purpose, giving a power to the guardian, whom he appointed by his will, to fix his terms of the dedication, and die without revoking his will, if the guardian takes possession of the third part of the inheritance, and dedicates it to that purpose, and limits the office of Mutevelli to himself, his children and his descendants, such dedication and the terms fixed by the guardian are valid and effect is given to them accordingly.

Nearest. ART. 156.—In the dedication, which the dedicator makes in favour of his nearest relations, the word " nearest " means the nearest relation of the dedicator both by consanguinity and degree.

It does not mean the nearest relation entitled to inherit or the male offspring.

Consequently, if one of the relations of the dedicator is nearer to him by consanguinity and degree than another, who is related according to the law of inheritance and as male offspring, the one nearest by consanguinity and degree is preferred.

E.g. When the granddaughter by a daughter and the great-grandson by a son co-exist, the granddaughter is preferred.

The great-grandson by the son is not preferred. Because the granddaughter by the daughter is nearer by consanguinity and degree than the great-grandson of the man by a son, notwithstanding that the great-grandson by a son is an heir and a relative through a male offspring, and that the granddaughter by a daughter is not heiress.

But when a grandson by a son and a granddaughter by a daughter co-exist, they both participate in the dedicated property because they are relations of the same degree.

The same rule applies in the case of an uncle on the mother's side and an uncle on the father's side.

ART. 157.—In relationship the nearness of degree is of force and not the strength of the relationship.

Consequently, if a dedicated property is limited in favour of the nearest relations, and there are two relations of the dedicator of the same degree, and of the one of them the relationship is strong and of the other the relationship is weak, they both participate in the dedicated property and the relation more strongly related is not preferred nor is the other precluded.

E.g. If a full blood brother of the dedicator and a half blood brother by the same mother co-exist, they both participate in the benefit of the dedicated property.

A full blood brother is not preferred to a half blood brother by the same mother by virtue of the full blood relationship.

ART. 158.—If anyone die, after he has limited the occupation of a house, which he dedicated to his wife on the condition that she is not to get married after his death, the occupation of the said house by his wife is interrupted if she afterwards gets married. *Dedication in favour of wife while she remains unmarried.*

In such a case the right to occupy the house does not revert to her by the death of her husband or by divorce.

Unless the dedicator explicitly direct that the right shall revert to his wife after the death of her husband or after divorce. In such a case such right reverts to her.

ART. 159.—If the dedicator limits the income of the property he dedicated, in favour of his poor neighbours, such income is spent for the poor neighbours of the quarter in which the dedicator is residing when the income is produced. *Poor neighbours.*

It does not particularly belong to the neighbours of the quarter in which he was residing when he made the dedication.

But they are spent for ever for the poor neighbours who belong to the quarter in which the dedicator was residing at his death.

E.g. If anyone dedicates a thing of his, and limits the income thereof to his poor neighbours, while residing in one quarter of Constantinople, and afterwards he changes his residence to another quarter, and while he is there the income is produced, such income is expended for his poor neighbours residing in the second quarter and not for those residing in the first quarter.

The same rule is applied also when he leaves the second quarter and changes his residence to another quarter.

But if the dedicator say anything when making the dedication, by which he limits the income to the poor neighbours residing in the quarter in which he resides, then the dedicated thing is limited solely in favour of the poor neighbours residing in the first quarter.

E.g. If the dedicator say at the time of making the dedication, that he limits the income of the property he dedicates to the poor neighbours of the quarter in which he resides at the time being, the income of the dedicated thing is expended for his poor neighbours residing in the first quarter, although the dedicator may have changed his residence to another quarter.

Freed slaves.

ART. 160.—Of the dedicated thing, which is limited to the freed slaves and their children, the freed female slaves and their children participate as well.

SECTION II.

Changing the terms of the dedication.

Change of terms of dedication not allowed (subject to 163).

ART. 161.—Even the dedicator himself cannot change the terms made in conformity with the Sacred Law of a valid and irrevocable act of dedication, and, if he does so, the change is not valid and of force.

Unless dedicator reserve power for himself to change once.

But if the dedicator at the time of the dedication reserve to himself the right to change afterwards the terms of the dedication, in such a case he can change the terms.

But when once the change is made this right ceases, and he cannot any more for the future change the terms.

Or more than once.

Unless the dedicator insert as a condition at the time of the act of dedication that he shall have the right to change the terms many times, in such a case, by one change the right does not cease, and it is applied many times.

Or for Mutevelli.

If the dedicator make a condition at the time of the dedication that after him the Mutevellis of the dedication shall have this right, even these also may in the prescribed manner change the terms.

Where power reserved change during last illness good.

ART. 162.—If the dedicator who has reserved for himself at the time of dedication, the right to change the terms of the dedication, change the terms of the dedication during his last illness, the change is valid and of force.

Dedicator can always change Mutevelli.

ART. 163.—The dedicator can change the terms about the office of Mutevelli, even if he did not reserve for himself at the time of dedication the right to change them, but it is necessary that the judge should give his approval.

E.g. If the dedicator, after he has appointed some stranger to the office of Mutevelli of the vaqf revoke, with the approval of the judge, this appointment, and limit the office of Mutevelli in favour of his children, the second limitation is carried out.

Construction.

ART. 164.—If a person who dedicates a property say : " Let the change of the vaqf depend on me," the expression is applied to a change of the terms of the vaqf.

It is never applied to the change of the vaqf property itself.

SECTION III.

*Matters in which the breach of the conditions imposed
by the dedicator is allowed.*

ART. 165.—In true dedications the breach of a condition imposed by the dedicator which is in conformity with the Sacred Law is not allowed.

But in cases of the greater benefit of the dedicated property, or of necessity, the breach of the condition of the dedicator is permitted with the approval of the judge.

E.g. If the dedicator make a term that the money of the dedicated property may be lent at 10%, the Mutevelli may, with the consent of the judge, lend the money at 15%, thus transgressing the condition made by the dedicator.

Again if a dedicator make a condition that some Ijare-i-vahide vaqf may not be let for a term exceeding one year, but a tenant is not found to take it for one year, and a three years' lease is asked for, the Mutevelli can, with the approval of the judge, let it for two or three years, and thus transgress the condition of the dedicator.

In general, the authority of the judge in respect of dedicated property depends on its usefulness.

Consequently, the direction of the judge which is beneficial under the circumstances, even if it is opposed to the condition of the dedicator, is valid and must be carried out.

But the direction of the judge, which is opposed to what is required by the circumstances, and hurtful, is not valid and not to be carried out.

E.g. When a tenant is found to take a dedicated property, which is directed not to be let for a longer term than one year, and no benefit can accrue to the vaqf by letting it for a longer period, if the judge decide that it should be let for longer than a year, this decision is not valid and is not to be carried out.

Marginal note: Breach of condition in accordance with Sacred Law not allowed except with the approval of the judge, for the benefit of dedication.

ART. 166.—The conditions of dedicators in the case of untrue dedications of the Takhsisat category need not be kept.

The Chief of the Mussulmans, taking care for the common benefit, if he thinks just, can alter the conditions of such dedications.

But if the objects, in favour of which these dedications exist, are of the sort which are supported by the Beit-ul-mal, then it is not allowed to abolish and annul them.

E.g. If the objects, in favour of which some dedication, specially dedicated is made, are the poor students in some school, and they are limited to the learning of useful sciences, since the said scholars study at the expense of the Beit-ul-mal, the abolition and annulling of that dedication cannot be allowed.

Marginal note: Conditions of untrue Takhsisat dedications need not be kept. *see* Articles 137, 138.

Marginal note: Unless object is a public one.

Terms not in
accordance
with the Sacred
Law need not
be carried out.

ART. 167.—Any term of a dedication which is not in conformity with the Sacred Law ceases to have force and is not to be carried out.

E.g. If the dedicator make a condition that the accounts of the vaqf are not to be examined by the judges, even if abuse of his trust on the part of the Mutevelli in the matters of the vaqf is shewn, and that the Mutevellis who are proved to have committed abuses in contravention of the terms of the dedication are not to be dismissed, this condition is not to be carried out.

Therefore, in case of necessity, the judges examine the accounts of that vaqf.

When abuse of his trust in the matters of the vaqf on the part of the Mutevelli is shewn, the judge dismisses him from his office.

Where
intention of
dedicator is un-
known custom
is followed.

ART. 168.—In matters in which the expressed intention of the dedicator is not known, ancient custom is to be followed.

Thus, in a case in which it is not possible to know in a matter relating to a vaqf the provision made by the dedicator, it is necessary that that should be done in relation to that matter, which, from the beginning, preceding Mutevellis of that vaqf did.

Consequently, it is not allowed in such a case to act contrary to the ancient custom.

E.g. When a dispute and contention have arisen about the office of Mutevelli or the expenses of a vaqf, and there is no executory deed of dedication recognized by the disputants, and it is not possible to shew by witnesses, what condition about the Mutevelliship and the expenses the dedicator made, it is necessary that that should be done which was done and decided upon in the ancient custom.

Where
beneficiary not
known benefit
is, by direction
of the judge,
given to the
poor.

ART. 169.—If it is impossible to find out the terms or the ancient custom concerning the object for which the income of an ancient dedication is to be expended, and for this reason the subject for which it is to be expended is not known, the income of that dedication, on the decision of the judge, is to be spent for the benefit of the poor and those without means.

Deed, not
proved and
acted on is not
carried out.

ART. 170.—The contents of a vaqfieh are not to be carried out if they are not proved and they have not been acted on from the beginning.

Deed of
dedication
differing from
conditions in
Defter
Khaqani.

ART. 171.—If there are found in the Defter Khaqani written conditions opposed to a vaqfieh which has been acted upon, that is to say, opposed to the terms of the vaqfieh in accordance with which, from the beginning, the dedication has been conducted, it is necessary that the said vaqfieh be carried out as before.

E.g. When in the vaqfieh of the dedicator which has been acted upon, it is clearly shewn that the income of the vaqf is limited in favour of the descendants of the dedicator from generation to generation, if in the Defter Khaqani there is no registered term " from generation to generation," but the dedication is limited absolutely in favour of his children and grandchildren, the writing in the Defter Khaqani is not to be carried out but the vaqfieh must be carried out as before.

Consequently, the income of that dedicated property is spent according to the vaqfieh for the benefit of all the offspring of the dedicator of whatever generation they may be, and not according to the document in the Defter Khaqani in favour of the children of the dedicator of the earlier generation.

In the contrary case, if a vaqfieh is produced which has not been acted upon and of which the contents have not been known, but, on the contrary, the Mutevellis have been used from the beginning to act according to the document in the Defter Khaqani, then it is necessary that they should continue to act in conformity with the document in the Defter Khaqani.

In one word, when in a matter relating to a vaqf, the vaqfieh and the document in the Defter Khaqani are opposed, in that matter, the document which is in accordance with ancient use is to be acted upon and not the other (*see note*).

ART. 172.—The authority of the terms of an act of dedication lies in the statement of the dedicator and not in the writing of the scribe.

Mistake in deed.

Consequently, when it is shewn in the way prescribed by the Sacred Law, that the conditions which the scribe wrote in the vaqfieh as the declaration of the dedicator are not in accordance with the terms which the dedicator stated and declared at the time of the dedication, the trust is carried out in conformity with the declaration of the dedicator and not according to what the scribe wrote.

E.g. When the dedicator at the time of the dedication declares that he limits the income of the vaqf in favour of his children and grandchildren, if the scribe by mistake write children instead of children and grandchildren, the dedicator's grandchildren share in accordance with his declaration.

The income is not limited in accordance with the writing of the scribe to his lawful children.

Again if the dedicator at the time of the dedication impose the condition that the change of the terms of the dedication depends upon himself, if the scribe did not write this condition in the vaqfieh, the declaration of the dedicator is carried out and he is empowered to change the terms of the dedication.

ART. 173.—If the dedicator records in the vaqfieh two inconsistent terms, which cannot be carried out together, the second term invalidates the first.

Consequently, the things required by the second term are carried out and not the things required by the first term.

E.g. If the dedicator put as a term in his vaqfieh that nothing is to be given out of the income of the property dedicated by him to his children and relations, and afterwards when fixing certain payments direct that a fixed sum of money is to be given to his children who have need and his relations, in the way of a grant for the recipient to offer up prayers in his behalf : since these two directions are opposed and the first is invalidated by the second, what is required by the second direction is carried out, and it is required that the payment fixed for his children who have need and his relations be given.

Again if the dedicator direct that the income of the vaqf is to be given to his children and grandchildren, but that no share shall be given to the second generation until the first is exhausted, and afterwards direct, that when a child of the first generation dies, his share shall be given to his children, the second direction is carried out.

Consequently, when one of the dedicator's children of the first generation dies, leaving children, and the child who died had a right to share in the income, his share is given to his children. It is not given according to the first direction in the vaqfieh to those of the first generation who together share the income.

ART. 174.—The possession of a right in respect of the dedicated property does not cease by its abandonment.

Thus a person who has according to the terms used by the dedicator a right out of the dedicated property does not lose that right by saying that he abandons it.

Consequently, he is entitled, after his abandonment, to demand that right.

E.g. If a person in whose favour the income of a dedicated property is limited, say that he abandons his right in respect of the income of that property, he can afterwards demand the income from it.

As regards the office of Mutevelli and the right of inhabiting a place, the rules above about income apply.

But if, at the time of the making by the dedicator of the dedication, the person in which favour it is made, be present and reject the thing dedicated, he is deprived of the appointed benefit from the vaqf, because in this case there was no assent made on his behalf.

In such a case, after the rejection, he cannot demand the appointed benefit.

Mention of this is made in Art. 47.

ART. 175.—In the case of a valid dedication of a benefit limited in favour of some object, another person outside the limitation of the dedicator cannot share. *Person, not entitled by the terms of the dedication, cannot share the benefit.*

E.g. When the dedicator dedicates a house, of which he limits the occupation if favour of a schoolmaster who according to the direction of the dedicator is the only one existing in a dedicated school, if another, contrary to the direction of the dedicator is appointed to the school, as second master, and take the Berat, he cannot share the occupation of that house with the first master.

ART. 176.—An absolute dedication relates to the income and not to the right to inhabit. *A dedication without restriction confers the income and not the right to inhabit.*

Consequently, when a house is dedicated, if the dedicator at the time of the dedication use unqualified words and does not say whether the beneficiary shall take the income or inhabit it, that house is let. The beneficiary enjoys the income and not the right to inhabit.

E.g. When one says that he dedicates his house to the master of such a school, but does not say anything to shew that it is directed that the schoolmaster should live in that house, or that it should be let and the income given to the schoolmaster, the Mutevelli lets the house and gives the income to the schoolmaster.

In such a case, the schoolmaster cannot, by reason that it was not made clear that the house should be let, prevent the letting of the house by the Mutevelli, and live in it.

ART. 177.—If one limit the income of a property dedicated by him in favour of the servants of one of the charitable institutions, such as a school and house of worship, but does not declare in what way the income shall be divided among the servants, it is divided amongst the servants equally. *If no direction, the division is equal (see Art. 149).*

There is not given to the higher servants a greater share than is given to the others.

CHAPTER V.

The different sorts of vaqf immovable property and certain rules relating to pious establishments.

ART. 178.—Immovable property made vaqf is of two categories :—

(*a*). Dedicated immovable properties which are dedicated upon the condition that their benefit is to be enjoyed without the necessity to make income out of them or to let them. *Non-income-bearing.*

These are called pious establishments (Muessesati Khairiye) (*see* Art. 16).

Income bearing.

(*b*) Dedicated immovable properties which are let out and delivered for the purpose of getting benefit from them, the rent and profit arising therefrom being limited for the benefit of some good object.

This second category is subdivided into three sorts :

(1). Into double rent vaqfs, Ijareteinlu Mevquf properties (*see* Art. 37).

(2). Into single rent vaqfs Ijare Vahidelu Mevquf properties (Art. 38).

(3). Into vaqfs called Muqata‘alu (Art. 39).

Pious establishments. Two sorts. Where rich participate.

ART. 179.—Pious establishments are of two sorts :—

(*a*). Pious establishments which are not limited only for the benefit of the poor, but it is allowed for the rich and poor to enjoy the benefit of them. Such as a house of worship, library, guest-chamber, fountain, well, bridge and common cemetery.

Where rich do not participate.

(*b*). Pious establishments which are limited for the benefit of the poor alone and it is not allowed that the rich should enjoy their benefit.

E.g. A poor house and vaqf hospitals for which it is directed that necessary things, such as food and drugs, should be given to the sick, and vaqf schools for which it is directed that the things required by the pupils are to be given from the income of the vaqf.

And in respect of such establishments, even if it is not declared by the dedicator that they are specially appointed for the benefit of the poor and this is not inserted in the vaqfieh, these belong only to the poor.

But if it is appointed and declared by the dedicator that the rich shall enjoy the benefit of such establishments with the poor, then the rich shall enjoy their benefit with the poor.

The dedication is not valid if it directs that the rich alone shall enjoy their benefits.

Descendants of dedicator preferred.

ART. 180.—In the case of the income of dedicated property which is limited absolutely in favour of the poor, the poor descendants of the dedicator are preferred to the poor children of others.

Again in the case of the occupation of a house limited in favour of the poor, the children and the descendants of the dedicator, who have need of it, are preferred to strangers who are poor.

Mussulman and non-Mussulman share equally.

ART. 181.—The income of dedicated property limited to supply the misfortunes and necessities of quarters and villages occupied by a mixed population of Mussulman and non-Mussulman, is expended towards the misfortunes and necessities of all the inhabitants, Mussulman and otherwise.

And this, whether the dedicator is Mussulman or not.

The same rule is applied also to the case of a dedicated property limited towards the misfortunes and needs of artificers, Mussulman and non-Mussulman.

ART. 182.—A person is not prevented, who wishes, out of his beneficence, to repair at his own expense a ruined pious foundation, although the dedication is wealthy. *Repair of pious foundation by stranger.*

ART. 183.—The persons having a right over a house which is dedicated to them for their occupation cannot divide it among themselves even if it is capable of division. *Division of dedicated house not allowed.*

ART. 184.—If the persons having a right over a house of which the occupation is dedicated to them are many, and the house is not adapted for occupation by all of them, they dwell in that house by turn. *Division of house by turns.*

ART. 185.—When the Mesjid in a community or village is found small and not able to hold the people, it is allowed to the inhabitants to pull it down and build in place of it, at their own expense, a large and firmer building than the first. *Rebuilding.*

ART. 186.—If a Mesjid is small and not able to hold the people, it is allowed to enlarge it by the addition of an income-bearing property dedicated to this Mesjid and adjacent to it. *Adding to.*

CHAPTER VI.

Mussaqafat and Mustaghelat vaqf properties held at double rent (Ijareteinli).

SECTION I.

The grant of Mussaqafat and Mustaghelat vaqf properties held at double rent, and the rules of inheritance with respect to them.

ART. 187.—When there is a question of letting and granting dedicated immovable properties at a double rent by the vaqf for the first time, to a person asking for it, a sum is taken in advance from that person on behalf of the vaqf, a rent payable in advance, called " Ijare-i-Muajele " approximate to the value of that property, and the property is handed to him on the condition that he shall pay at the expiration of each year a small sum called " Ijare-i-Muejele." *Letting of Ijareteinli.*

ART. 188.—The raqabe of Ijaretein vaqf immovable properties and the property itself belong to the vaqf, and the tasarruf of them to the lessees at double rent. *Ownership belongs to dedication.*

They possess such Ijaretein vaqfs as long as they live. *Right of use to lessee.*

Inheritance when right not extended.

When they die, they are transferred to their male and female children equally, and without payment of the equivalent value (*see* Law about inheritance of Ijaretein vaqfs, 4 Rejeb, 1292, and 15 Zilkade, 1292 and note).

If they die without children, they belong to the vaqf, by reason of their being left without owner as they are transmissible only to the children.

Inheritance when dedicator directs that they should be inherited like mulk.

But if the dedicator directs in the vaqfieh made by him, that Mussaqafat and Mustaghelat Ijaretein properties should be transferred to the heirs of the persons possessing them, in the same way as pure mulk properties are transferred, in such a case such properties are transferred, after the death of the person possessing them, to his heirs in proportion to the hereditary share each is entitled to.

Inheritance when right extended.

Also, in accordance with the Imperial Law issued and published on the second of Zilkade, 1285, the Mussaqafat and Mustaghelat Ijaretein properties, of which the hereditary right is extended at the request and wish of their owner, are transferred first, to his male and female children in equal shares, as formerly, and second, to the grandchildren of the deceased owner.

That is to say, when a person, being the tenant of an Ijaretein property, of which the hereditary right has been extended, dies without leaving any children, but leaving only grandchildren, notwithstanding that such grandchildren were the issue of different children of his, such properties are transferred to all of them equally.

E.g. If the tenant of an Ijaretein property, of which the hereditary right has been extended dies without children but leaving five children of a predeceased son and a child of a predeceased daughter, such property is regarded as consisting of six shares, five of which are transferred to the five children of the deceased son, and one to the only child of the deceased daughter.

Or if he leaves two children of a predeceased son, three children of another predeceased son and four children of a predeceased daughter, such property is considered as consisting of nine shares and one share is transferred to each of them.

When extended great grandchildren do not inherit.

ART. 189.—Ijaretein immovable properties, of which the hereditary right is extended, pass only to the grandchildren and not to more remote descendants.

Consequently the great grandchildren are not entitled to inherit any Ijaretein properties of their great grandfather.

E.g. If the son and the son of the son of the tenant of an Ijaretein property, of which the hereditary right is extended, die, and afterwards the owner dies leaving a great-grandson, such property is not transferred to the great-grandson.

ART. 190.—The children of male and female children, who die while their father and mother are living, are looked upon as children and the share which would pass to their parents if they were living, from their grandfather and grandmother is transferred to them.

(a). That is to say, if the tenant of an Ijaretein property, of which the hereditary right is extended, die leaving children and grandchildren, the issue of a predeceased child, then the predeceased children are supposed to be living and the shares which would have passed to them, if alive, on the division of the property, pass to their children.

E.g. If the tenant of an Ijaretein property, of which the hereditary right is extended, dies leaving two sons, one daughter and three children of another son who is dead, the three shares of this property pass to the two sons and the daughter and the other share passes in equal proportions to the three children of the predeceased son.

Or, if he dies leaving a son and a son of a predeceased daughter, half of that property is transferred to the son and the other half to the son of his daughter. Or, if he dies leaving three sons, one daughter, three children of another predeceased son and two children of another predeceased daughter, in such a case the property is looked upon as consisting of six shares, of which four are transferred to the three sons and the son of the daughter,—each taking one share—one share to the three children of the deceased son and one share to the two children of the deceased daughter.

(b). When the person possessing an Ijaretein property of which the hereditary right is extended, dies leaving children or grandchildren, the surviving husband or wife is not entitled to have the property transferred to him or her

(c). It passes to the parents.

That is to say, when the owner of an Ijaretein property, of which the hereditary right is extended, dies without leaving children or grandchildren, but leaving father and mother, then that property passes in equal shares to his father and mother.

If he only has a father, the whole property is transferred to him, or if he only has a mother, it is all transferred to her.

If besides the father and mother, or either of them, a husband or wife co-exist, then one-fourth of the property is transferred to the husband or wife, as the case may be.

E.g. When the owner of an Ijaretein property, of which the hereditary right is extended, dies without leaving children and grandchildren, but leaving wife, father and mother, then one-fourth of that property is transferred to the wife and three-fourths equally to the parents. Or, if he leaves wife and father, then one-fourth is transferred to the wife,

Margin notes:

Children of deceased children take the share of their parents.

Children and grandchildren inherit to exclusion of husband or wife.

Parents when entitled to inherit.

and three-fourths to his father. Or, if he leaves wife and mother, one-fourth is transferred to the wife and three-fourths to his mother.

Or, when a wife, while in possession of an Ijaretein property, of which the hereditary right is extended, dies without leaving children or grandchildren, but leaving husband, father and mother, then one-fourth of that property is transferred to the husband and three-fourths to her parents equally. Or, if she leaves husband and father, then one-fourth of it is transferred to the husband and three-fourths to her father. Or, if she leaves husband and mother, then one-fourth is transferred to the husband and the residue to her mother.

(*d*). It is transferred to brother and sister of the full blood.

That is to say, if the owner of an Ijaretein property of which the hereditary right is extended, dies without leaving children, grandchildren or parents, but leaving a full blood brother and a full blood sister, then that property is transferred to them equally.

If he leaves only a full blood brother, then all that property is transferred to him.

Or, if he leaves a full blood sister, then that property is all transferred to her. The transfer is carried out equally, whatever may be the number of the full blood brothers and sisters.

(*e*). It is transferred to a brother and sister having the same father.

When the owner of an Ijaretein property of which the hereditary right is extended, dies without leaving any children, grandchildren, father, mother and brother of the full blood, but leaving only brothers and sisters having the same father, then the property is transferred to them equally.

In such a case, when there is a husband or wife, one-fourth is transferred to them and the residue to the brother having the same father.

The details set out in respect of full blood brothers are applied to those having the same father as well.

(*f*). It passes to the brothers and sisters having the same mother.

That is to say, if the owner of an Ijaretein property of which the hereditary right is extended, dies without leaving children, grandchildren, parents, brothers of full blood and brothers having the same father only, but leaving brothers and sisters having the same mother, then that property is transferred to them equally.

In such a case, the husband or wife receives one-fourth share.

The details aforesaid also apply to brothers having the same mother.

(g). It passes from husband to wife and *vice versa*.

That is to say, if the owner of an Ijaretein property, of which the hereditary right is extended, dies without leaving any heir of any of the above-mentioned degrees entitled to inherit, but leaving only a wife, then that property all passes to her.

In case there are many wives, the property passes to all of them equally.

Or, if a woman, being the possessor of an Ijaretein property, of which the hereditary right is extended, dies without leaving any heir, within the degrees of relationship above-mentioned, entitled to inherit that property, but leaving a husband only, then that property passes to her husband.

In order that a husband or wife should be entitled to inherit, as above stated, it must be proved, that he or she, is entitled to inherit pure mulk properties.

That is to say, a husband or wife, who is an heir or heiress in pure mulk estates, is entitled to inherit Ijaretein immovable properties and he or she, who is not an heir or heiress in pure mulk properties, is not entitled to inherit Ijaretein immovable properties.

Consequently, if after a marriage is contracted, either of the spouses dies before the consummation of the marriage, the surviving spouse is entitled to inherit.

Also, if after a person has divorced his wife by a revocable divorce, either of the spouses dies within the time during which the wife is not allowed to marry again, (iddet, 100 days), the surviving spouse is entitled to inherit.

But if either of the spouses die after the expiration of iddet, (100 days), the surviving spouse is not entitled to inherit.

In case the divorce is final, notwithstanding that either of the spouses dies within the time of iddet, (100 days), the surviving spouse is not entitled to inherit. But if a person during mortal illness divorces a wife by a final divorce without application having been made by her, and dies before the iddet of his wife expires, the wife is entitled to inherit.

ART. 191.—The Ijaretein properties of an absentee, as to whom it is not known whether he is alive or dead or where he is are not transferred to his heirs unless his death is either in fact or legally proved.

ART. 192.—If the dead bodies of any two relations are discovered in a wrecked ship, drowned, or buried under the ruins of a building which has fallen down, or in a building which has been burnt and it is not known which of the two died first, such relations, inasmuch as they cannot inherit the one from the other as regards the mulk estates, are not entitled to inherit Ijaretein properties one from the other, but such properties pass to their living heirs.

E.g. If the owner of an Ijaretein property dies together with his son by being drowned, buried alive, or burnt as aforesaid, and it is not known which of the two died first and the remaining living children of the person, so dying with his son, take possession of that property by virtue of inheritance, the children of the son, who died at the same time as his father, cannot take any share out of that property, alleging as a reason that the said share passed to their father from their grandfather.

Mahlul.

If the owner of an Ijaretein property, of which the hereditary right is extended, dies without leaving anybody entitled to any inheritance, that property belongs to the vaqf as unoccupied.

But if a person has agreed that an Ijaretein property should be granted to him, on the condition that he is to maintain the person so granting it during his lifetime and such a condition is inserted on the Land Registry title by leave of the Mutevelli and the grantee afterwards dies, while the grantor is still living, leaving no heir entitled to inherit, then that property is not looked upon as unoccupied, but by the consent of the Mutevelli is given to the grantor.

N.B. In the case of non-Mussulman tenants of Ijaretein vaqfs, where the property does not escheat to the vaqf the Law of Inheritance in Cyprus is amended by the Act XX. of 1895.

Section II.

Obstacles to inheritance.

Difference of religion.

Art. 193.—The difference of religion which exists between a Mussulman and a non-Mussulman prevents the transmission by inheritance.

Consequently, at the death of a Mussulman, his Ijaretein Mussaqafat and Mustaghelat vaqfs do not pass to his non-Mussulman children and relations.

Also, at the death of a non-Mussulman, his Ijaretein Mussaqafat and Mustaghelat vaqfs do not pass to his Mussulman children and relations.

But the difference of religion, which exists between two non-Mussulmans does not prevent the property passing.

E.g. The Ijaretein Mussaqafat and Mustaghelat vaqfs pass from a Christian to a Jew and *vice versa*.

Consequently, when a Jew being an Ottoman subject while he is the owner of an Ijaretein property, die leaving two children, who are Ottoman subjects of whom one is Christian and the other a Jew and the Christian wishes to take possession of half of that property by right of inheritance, the Jew cannot contend that he is entitled to possess that property exclusively for the reason that their father was a Jew and his brother is a Christian and that, therefore, he is not entitled to inherit that property. The same rule is applied when the person who dies is a Christian.

Also, when a Jew, being an Ottoman subject, while he is the owner of an Ijaretein property, dies leaving a Christian child who is an Ottoman subject, and that child wishes to take possession of the property by right of inheritance the Mutevelli cannot prevent such child from inheriting for the reason that the father was a Jew and the child a Christian and that the property does not pass to the child and is unoccupied (Mahlul).

The same rules apply also in case the deceased is a Christian and the child a Jew.

ART. 194.—The fact that people are subjects of different Governments, that is to say, difference of nationality, prevents inheritance. **Differences of nationality.**

That is to say, when a Mussulman, who is an Ottoman subject dies, his Ijaretein property does not pass to his children and relations who have a foreign nationality.

Also, when a Mussulman, who is a foreign subject, dies while in possession of an Ijaretein property, in conformity with the Law, by which right of ownership is granted to foreigners, that property does not pass to the heirs who are Ottoman subjects.

If an Ottoman subject, being the owner of an Ijaretein property acquires a foreign nationality, without obtaining an official permission, the properties in his name, being unoccupied, belong to the vaqf and do not pass to his children and relations who would otherwise be entitled to inherit.

But if he acquires a foreign nationality after he has received an official permission, then the following rules are to be observed :—

If the State of which he acquires the nationality, has agreed and signed the protocol dealing with the rights of ownership of foreign subjects, his Ijaretein properties are not looked upon as unoccupied, but they belong to him as formerly.

But if the State, of which he acquires the nationality, has not agreed to and signed the protocol dealing with the rights of ownership of foreign subjects, in such a case the property is looked upon as unoccupied.

ART. 195.—Homicide is a bar to inheritance. **Homicide when a bar.**

E.g. A person, who has killed his own father is barred from inheriting Ijaretein Mussaqafat and Mustaghelat vaqfs which his father possessed in his lifetime.

F2

Upon this matter, the word "homicide" means and includes a homicide, the consequence of which is deprivation of inheritance in mulk estates.

A homicide, the consequence of which is not the deprivation of inheritance in mulk estates is not a bar to the right of inheritance in Ijaretein immovable properties, (*compare* Land Law, Art. 108).

Slavery. ART. 196.—Slavery is a bar to inheritance.

E.g. If a person, while owner of an Ijaretein property, die leaving children, who are slaves, that property does not pass to them.

Shares which have lapsed through disability. ART. 197.—If anyone being entitled to inherit is deprived of the inheritance by reason of any of the above causes, the share which he would have inherited but for that obstacle is not looked upon as unoccupied and it passes to the other heirs.

E.g. If a non-Mussulman, who is an Ottoman subject, being the owner of an Ijaretein property, die leaving two non-Mussulman sons, of whom one is an Ottoman subject and the other a foreigner, in such a case the property passes to his son who is an Ottoman subject exclusively.

The half share of that property is not considered as unoccupied because the other son is a foreigner.

Also, if, for example, one of the three children of some-one, who possesses an Ijaretein property kills him in a way which results in the deprivation of inheritance, his other two children take possession of that property by inheritance.

The third of his property is not looked upon as unoccupied for the reason that one of his children is his murderer.

N.B. In the case of non-Mussulman tenants of Ijaretein vaqfs in Cyprus, when the property has not escheated to the vaqf, the Law as to disabilities of heirs is amended by the Act XX. of 1895 (*see* Sections, 12, 13, 15, 16 and 17).

SECTION III.
Final alienation (Feragh-i-qati').

Power to alienate. ART. 198.—The Ijaretein tenants of Mussaqafat and Mustaghelat vaqfs may alienate them to another either on payment of an equivalent value or gratis.

N.B. As to power to alienate part of an Ijaretein vaqf see Art. 238; as to alienation by joint owners, see Art. 240.

Alienation how made. ART. 199.—An alienation is made by a proposal and acceptance.

Permission of Mutevelli necessary. But the permission of the Mutevelli of the vaqf to which the property alienated belongs is required, in order that the alienation may be valid. Any alienation made without permission of the Mutevelli is not valid or of force.

Consequently, the alienor and alienee can, if either of them wish, revoke an alienation which is made without the permission of the Mutevelli.

And if the alienee die, the alienor is owner of the property alienated.

And if the alienor die, the property passes to his heirs who are entitled to inherit.

But if he has no heirs entitled to inherit, the property belongs to the vaqf as an unoccupied property would.

In one word, an alienation made between the alienor and the alienee without the permission of the Mutevelli is invalid.

ART. 200.—If the Ijaretein tenant of Mussaqafat and Mustaghelat vaqf property finally alienates it to another, with the permission of the Mutevelli, and the title is not prepared, the alienor cannot revoke the alienation for the reason that the title has not yet been prepared. *Alienation complete though title not prepared.*

ART. 201.—A subsequent condition does not affect a previous transaction. *Conditions subsequently made and contemporary conditions.*

Consequently, when a person alienates his Ijaretein property to another with the permission of the Mutevelli, finally and unconditionally, for a fixed sum of money paid, if after some time the alienee promise to the alienor that he will give back and convey that property to him as soon as the value thereof is repaid to him, and if he gives him even a document to that effect, the person making such promise is not bound to carry it out.

That is to say, if the alienee do give and alienate back to him that property according to his promise, the transaction in good, otherwise no judge can force him to do so.

But if such an agreement was made between the alienor and the alienee before the alienation, which was made in consequence of that agreement, in such a case the alienee is bound to give and alienate back to the alienor the property alienated, according to the agreement.

ART. 202.—If a person, after he alienate his Ijaretein property to another gratis and unconditionally, with the permission of the Mutevelli, repents, he is not entitled to demand the price from the alienee or to ask the alienee to return that property to him. *Gift with permission of Mutevelli final.*

Also, if anyone, while in good health, alienates his Ijaretein property to another gratis, with the permission of the Mutevelli, and afterwards dies without leaving anybody entitled to inherit, the Mutevelli is not entitled to interfere with the property alienated, or ask for a Muajele rent from the alienee.

ART. 203.—The alienor must be of full age and of sound mind. *Alienor must be of full age and sound mind.*

Consequently, an alienation made by an infant, lunatic, or a person who has reached his second childhood is not valid or of force.

Force.

ART. 204.—In alienating a property, the consent of the alienor is required.

Consequently, an alienation made under the influence of force is not valid.

Alienation by exchange.

ART. 205.—The alienation of Ijaretein Mussaqafat and Mustaghelat vaqfs by exchange for another is allowed.

E.g. If anyone alienate his Ijaretein house taking in exchange another Ijaretein house held by another, such an alienation is allowed. But if the houses exchanged belong to different vaqfs, in order that the exchange be valid, it is required that the Mutevelli of both the vaqfs should give permission for that purpose.

Alienation before the judge.

ART. 206.—If anyone alienates his Ijaretein property to another before a judge and the judge reduce the agreement made for such alienation into writing, the alienation is not valid or of force unless the Mutevelli of that vaqf property grant permission to alienate.

But in a case in which, after the completion of a trial, it becomes necessary that the Ijaretein property of one of the litigants should be alienated to another, if the judge, in accordance with the articles contained in a special chapter, appoint temporarily an agent of the Mutevelli for that proceeding and the alienation is carried out with his permission, then such an alienation is valid and of force.

Revocation of agreement to alienate.

ART. 207.—If a person agree to alienate his Ijaretein property to another and afterwards repent of the agreement and decline to confirm the alienation in the presence of the Mutevelli, he is not forced to carry out the alienation.

Penalty on rescission not enforceable.

ART. 208.—If a person agree to alienate his Ijaretein property to another and it is agreed between the contracting parties that the party revoking the agreement is to pay to the other a fixed sum of money in case he repents of the bargain, such an undertaking is of no value whatever.

Consequently, if one of the contracting parties revokes that agreement, he cannot be adjudged to pay to the other that sum of money.

SECTION IV.

Alienation made by a sick person.

Alienation during last illness.

ART. 209.—If a person, during the illness of which he dies, alienates vaqf Mustaghelat held in Ijaretein with the permission of the Mutevelli and afterwards he dies, the following rules are to be observed :—

If there exist any heirs of the alienor entitled to inherit, the alienation is valid and of force. But if such heirs do not exist, then the alienation is not valid and of force, and the alienated Mustaghelat belongs to the vaqf as unoccupied (*compare* Mejellé, Arts. 394 and 877).

In this case if the purchaser has paid anything as price to the vendor, he recovers it from the estate of the vendor.

ART. 210.—If a person suffering from a chronic disease, which lasts for over a year, after his condition changes and his disease becomes worse, sells his Ijaretein property to another, by leave of the Mutevelli, and after a few days dies without leaving any heir entitled to inherit, such an alienation is not valid. *Sale by chronic invalid.*

Consequently, that property belongs to the dedication, as unoccupied. But if he alienates that property before his condition is changed and his disease gets worse, in such a case the alienation is valid (Art. 1595, Mejellé).

ART. 211.—If a person during his illness of which he dies alienate by leave of the Mutevelli his vaqf Mustaghel, held by Ijaretein, to one of his heirs entitled to inherit, such an alienation is valid and of force (*compare* Art. 393, Mejellé). *Alienation during last illness to heir.*

Consequently, in such a case, the other heirs entitled to inherit cannot interfere with the property alienated, alleging that they do not approve of the alienation, on the ground that it was made in the course of an illness of which the alienor died.

E.g. If a person having three children die after he has alienated to one of them, by leave of the Mutevelli, his vaqf Mustaghel, held by Ijaretein, during the illness of which he died, his other two children cannot interfere with that property.

ART. 212.—When a sick person wishes to alienate his Ijaretein property to another, his heirs, who are entitled to inherit, cannot prevent him from making the alienation. *Alienation by invalid.*

ART. 213.—When a sick person, who has no heir, desires to alienate his Ijaretein property to another, the Mutevelli cannot refuse him the leave required for that purpose, saying " his illness may prove fatal and I don't grant leave for the alienation before he recovers." *Alienation by invalid who has no heir.*

Because the disease is proved to be fatal by the death of the sick person and it cannot be proved before his death.

But if the sick person die after the alienation is made without recovering from the illness from which he was suffering, and the disease is thus ascertained to have been fatal, it is proved that the alienation is invalid, and then, even if the Mutevelli had granted leave for the alienation in writing, such Mutevelli takes the property alienated from the hands of the alienee in order that it should be converted into Mahlul (unoccupied). In such a case, if the alienee had paid the price of the alienated property to the alienor, he takes the same out of the property left by the alienor.

SECTION V.

Guardians and alienations by and to the guardians of persons under disability.

Alienation by guardian.

ART. 214.—The natural guardian of an infant, being in good credit, or other voluntary guardian or a guardian who has been appointed, can, by leave of a judge and the permission of the Mutevelli, sell the vaqf property of an infant to another for its value, if the circumstances are such as are required by the Sheri' Law for the permission of such sale (*e.g.* if the property is in a state of ruin and the income is not equal to the expenses, or if there is necessity to raise money for the maintenance of the infant), provided that it is made clear, by the evidence of persons possessing competent knowledge, to the satisfaction of a judge, that the sale of the property to another will be for good reason and for the benefit of the infant and for its value.

In such a case, after the property has been so alienated, when the infant comes of age, he cannot claim that property back.

But if there is no lawful reason, the natural guardian cannot alienate that property to another and if he do so the alienation is not legal or of force.

In such a case, therefore, an infant, after he becomes of age, can, by leave of the Mutevelli, demand and take back that property from the alienee.

The same rule applies in the case of a lunatic or a man who has reached his second childhood.

Purchase for infant.

ART. 215.—The natural guardian can agree to buy an Ijaretein property on behalf of an infant by leave of a judge and the consent of the Mutevelli for its value, if it is proved that such a purchase is beneficial to the infant.

The same rule applies in the case of a lunatic or a person who has reached his second childhood.

Guardian cannot buy infant's property.

ART. 216.—A guardian cannot buy for himself an Ijaretein property which belongs to an infant of whom he is the guardian.

But a guardian, after he alienates that property to another for reasons recognized by the Sheri' Law and by the approval of a judge and the consent of the Mutevelli, at a price equal to its value, can buy it for himself from the person who first bought it.

Upon this subject, the same rule applies to the natural guardian as well.

Repairs by guardian for infant.

ART. 217.—When it is necessary to repair an Ijaretein property belonging to an infant, if it is proved that that property will be entirely ruined and the infant damaged, if it is left in the condition in which it is then, and not repaired, and that the repairs to be made out of the estate of the infant will be beneficial to him, the natural or other guardian can repair the same by leave of a judge out of the estate of the infant at a reasonable cost.

In such a case, if the infant die, the heirs cannot disapprove of the expenditure caused to be made by the natural guardian in the manner aforesaid.

The same rule applies in the case of a lunatic and of a person who has reached his second childhood.

SECTION VI.

Conditional alienation.

ART. 218.—The conditions which render an act of sale (Bey') defective, also render defective an agreement for alienation (feragh).

Defective alienation.

That is to say, when a person wants to alienate his Ijaretein property in the presence of the Mutevelli, if he alienates it under a defective condition which is agreed to by the alienee, and the Mutevelli grants leave under this condition, such an alienation is defective. But if the alienation is agreed upon between the alienor and the alienee under a defective condition, and afterwards, without the said condition being mentioned before the Mutevelli, the alienor alienates that property by a final alienation, and the Mutevelli grant his permission for the alienation as final, such an alienation is not defective.

The agreement entered into between the alienor and the alienee is looked upon as invalid.

ART. 219.—A condition providing for the maintenance of the alienor up to his death does not render an alienation, made gratis, defective.

Condition to maintain alienor does not render alienation defective.

That is to say, if a person alienates his Ijaretein property on the condition that he is to be maintained up to his death, and the alienee receive the property under the said condition, and the Mutevelli grants leave for the alienation upon these terms, such an alienation is valid and the condition of force.

Consequently, in such a case the alienor cannot revoke the alienation, and claim and recover the alienated property from the alienee, as long as he is willing to maintain the alienor.

But if the alienee does not carry out the said condition by maintaining the alienor, then such alienor is entitled to revoke the alienation and seek and recover from the alienee, with the approval of the Mutevelli, the property alienated (Imperial Irade, dated 28 Rejeb, 1296, Mejellé, Art. 855).

SECTION VII.

Option to rescind for defect, on sight, for excessive damage and fraud.

Option to to rescind for defect.

ART. 220.—In the alienation of an Ijaretein property the right of option for defect and option on sight are of force.

That is to say, if anyone, upon dedicated property which is alienated to him by another, observe an old defect, which would, according to the Sacred Law, cause the rejection thereof, he can return the same to the alienor, with the consent of the Mutevelli, by virtue of his right of option from defect.

Until a person has received the dedicated property, which is alienated to him by another, without his seeing it, he is entitled to the right of option.

When he sees it he can, if he likes, rescind the sale with the consent of the Mutevelli, or accept it (Arts. 320 and 336, Mejellé).

Option excessive injury without fraud.

ART. 221.—If at the alienation of vaqf Mussaqafat and Mustaghelat held by Ijaretein excessive damage occurs without fraud, the person who sustains the loss, whether he is the alienor or the alienee, cannot rescind the alienation (*compare* Art. 356, Mejellé).

But if the natural or appointed guardian of infants alienate such a dedicated property at a price excessively low, even if there is no fraud, the alienation is not valid (Art. 356, Mejellé).

Consequently, an infant, when he becomes of age, can claim and recover that property.

The same rules apply also in the case of a lunatic and of a person who has reached his second childhood.

Also if such a dedicated property is alienated by the Muteveli at a price excessively low, even if there is no fraud, such an alienation is not valid (Mejellé, Art. 356).

Also if a mandatory to effect an alienation alienate the property at an excessively low price, even if there be no fraud, the alienation is not valid as will be explained in a special chapter (*see* Chapter XII.).

Excessive loss by fraud.

ART. 222.—If it is proved that the alienor, in alienating a property, defrauded the alienee or *vice versa*, and that there is excessive damage, the person who sustains the damage can dissolve the alienation.

E.g. If a person say to another " my Ijaretein workshop, which is situated at such a place, is let at a monthly rent of 500 *cp.* and its equivalent value is 100,000 *cp.* and I give it you for that sum," and the other having trusted his words take it, with the Mutevelli's consent, at the price of 100,000, if it is afterwards proved that that workshop is let for 300 *cp.* per month and the price thereof is hardly 70,000 *cp.*, the person receiving the same, with the Mutevelli's consent, rescinds the alienation and takes back from the alienor the price which he paid.

Also when a person, addressing himself to an unskilled man, who is the possessor of an Ijaretein property say that that property is hardly worth 50,000 *cp.* and no more, and thus persuade him to alienate it to him at that price, and such unskilled man alienate the said property to the person who persuaded him, with the consent of the Mutevelli ; if it is afterwards proved by the evidence of trustworthy and impartial experts that the value of that property is 80,000 *cp.* and that there was fraud and excessive damage in the alienation, the alienor can, with the consent of the Mutevelli, rescind the alienation and return the price to the alienee and take the property back.

Section VIII.
Price of alienation and right of recovery.

ART. 223.—If a person alienates and delivers vaqf Mussaqafat or Mustaghelat held by Ijaretein to another, by leave of the Mutevelli, on the condition that a fixed sum of money be paid, and the purchaser does not pay the money, the alienor can demand the purchase money from the alienee and bring an action. *(Recovery of price.)*

In such a case, if the person, who bought the property die before paying the purchase money, the alienor can claim and recover the purchase money from the estate of the alienee.

ART. 224.—The purchase money is inherited in the same way as other things are. *(Price— inheritance of.)*

That is to say, if a person alienate and deliver his Ijaretein property at a fixed price and he die before receiving from the alienee the price thereof, such purchase money is taken from the alienee and, being added to the estate of the deceased, is divided among the heirs in proprotion to the hereditary share of each.

Consequently, the heirs of the alienor, who are entitled to inherit, cannot contend that the purchase money of such dedicated properties goes to them only, as those properties would have gone, and preclude the heirs not entitled to inherit such properties from receiving their lawful share out of the purchase money.

In general, the purchase money is looked upon as part of the estate of the deceased and is governed by the rules of the Sheri' Law, which apply to the rest of the estate (*see* note).

ART. 225.—If anybody appears and claims part of an Ijaretein property which another person has bought, for *(Return of price where ouster.)*

which he has paid the purchase money, and, after proving his right he recovers such part and a judgment is given for that, the alienee returns the property to the alienor, with the consent of the Mutevelli, and takes back from him the purchase money.

Where Mutevelli grants and a third party recovers the property.

ART. 226.—If, after a Mutevelli of a vaqf has alienated to some person a property, as part of the Mustaghelat of the vaqf of which he is Mutevelli for a sum paid as Muajele and a sum to be paid as Muejele, a third person come forward alleging that that property is his and proves his action, and after taking an oath himself, recovers the property and a judgment is given then, the alienee takes back from the Mutevelli the Muajele rent.

SECTION IX.

Partition, division and distribution of benefit derived from a dedicated property.

Partition allowed, when property divisible and beneficial to dedication.

ART. 227.—The partition of an Ijaretein property held in common among the joint owners is allowed, subject to two conditions (1131 and 1139 Mej., Art. 183).

(*a*) That the property should be divisible, that is to say, each joint owner to be able to enjoy the benefit belonging to him after division.

(*b*) The division should be more beneficial to the dedication.

Consequently, the partition of Ijaretein properties which are indivisible or of which the division is injurious to the dedication, is not valid.

After these conditions have been ascertained and proved, it is also an indispensable condition that the partition be made by leave of the Mutevelli.

Consequently, the partition of Ijaretein properties made without the leave of the Mutevelli, is not valid or of force.

When division not beneficial.

ART. 228.—It is looked upon as damage to the dedicated property caused by the division, if after the division a part of a dedicated building site remains without a way to it, or after the division of a large dedicated site into small parts, the value of the property is decreased and the former income diminished.

Partition may be enforced.

ART. 229.—In case of Ijaretein properties held in common and capable of division and of which the division is beneficial to the dedication, the division is carried out compulsorily.

That is to say, if some of the joint owners of such property apply for its division, and some of them do not consent, the judge orders that the building and building site of that property be locally inspected, and valued by persons who have full knowledge of buildings, in the presence of the parties interested and of the Mutevelli. If after such inspection it is proved by the evidence of experts that that property is capable of division amongst the joint owners, in a way beneficial to the dedication, then the judge, without taking into consideration the consent of the persons not consenting to the division, divides that property, with the approval of the Mutevelli, amongst the joint owners, by lot, in proportion to their shares, and fixes and separates them by placing distinctive marks on each share.

ART. 230.—If some of the joint owners of Ijaretein properties, held in common, are infants, lunatic or persons who have reached their second childhood, the partition is carried out through their natural or appointed guardians or representatives (Art. 1128, Mejellé). *Partition may be made by guardian when beneficial to infant, &c.*

But it is required that such partition should be beneficial to the dedication and still more beneficial to the infant, lunatic or person who has reached his second childhood.

ART. 231.—Dedicated ghediks held in common and possessed in Ijaretein are not capable of partition according to the Civil Law. *When there are ghediks.*

Also when, within Ijaretein properties, there are ghediks dedicated by a final dedication, the partition of such Ijaretein properties, within which such ghediks are found is prohibited, unless such ghediks are abolished by an Imperial decree and through the Mutevelli, or, unless they are included in the portion taken by one of the joint owners, by their consent.

ART. 232.—A compulsory partition in respect of a number of Ijaretein properties held in common, by joining them together for the purpose of division, is not enforced. *Properties cannot be joined for partition.*

E.g. While two persons hold some Ijaretein properties in common and in equal shares, if one of the joint owners ask that such properties might be partitioned by joining them together for the purposes of division and giving one property to one and the other to the other joint owner, and the other joint owner refuses to agree to such partition, the judge cannot compel the dissenting joint owner to agree to such partition.

ART. 233.—The partition must be just (Mejellé, 1127). *Partition rescinded if excessive damage.*

That is to say, the share to be allotted to each of the joint owners, whether in a voluntary partition or partition under the order of a judge, must be equal to the right which each joint owner has upon the property to be partitioned, and not excessively deficient.

Consequently, after the joint owners have divided their Ijaretein properties, which are held in common, either

62   The Laws of Evqaf.

under the decision of the judge or by their mutual consent, and leave of the Mutevelli, if one of them allege and prove that there is excessive damage done to him by the share allotted him, the division is rescinded.

But if after the division is made the joint owners release each other from the effect of an action respecting the division, in such a case an action about damage is not heard. Nevertheless, when there are persons under disability amongst the joint owners such as infants, lunatics or persons who have reached their second childhood, and a partition is made by their natural or appointed guardians or protectors, actions in respect of damage existing in the share of persons under disability are heard, even if their natural or appointed guardians or protectors have given a release in the manner aforesaid. Because the release given by the natural or appointed guardians or protectors of persons under disability is not valid.

Equalization of shares by payment allowed if both parties consent. ART. 234.—Although the partition amongst the joint owners of an Ijaretein property held in common, of which the division is impossible without the addition of a sum of money, is allowed by the consent of the joint owners and by leave of the Mutevelli, yet one cannot be forced if he does not consent. Thus ; when there is a dissent, the property cannot be divided compulsorily.

When, at the division of an Ijaretein house owned by two persons in common in undivided and equal shares, the value of one of the shares of the building is higher than the other, if one of the joint owners, wishing to take the share having the higher value, propose to the other to have that house divided and offer a fixed sum of money in order to make up for the deficiency on the other share, and the other joint owner agree to it, and the division is beneficial to the dedication, in such a case such joint owners can divide that house with the consent of the Mutevelli.

But if one of the joint owners refuses, the judge cannot force him to agree to such division.

Division of profits when property is indivisible. ART. 235.—When amongst the joint owners of Ijaretein income-bearing properties which are incapable of division, or of which the division is injurious to the dedication, a litigation or dispute arises as to the possession of the said properties, while in an undivided condition, and some of the joint owners claim the division of the benefit derived from the property and some refuse it, the judge, without taking into consideration the dissent of the person refusing, with the Mutevelli's consent, decides that the property should be possessed in turn (*see* Circular 10, Shaban, 1296, after the occupation of Cyprus, I. Nicolaides, 1241).

ART. 236.—The time elapsed, before the division of the benefit, cannot be set off against the turn for enjoying it.

E.g. When one of the two joint owners of an Ijaretein house has lived in it exclusively for a time before the division of the benefit, and afterwards, with their mutual consent, or by the decision of the judge and the consent of the Mutevelli, they agree to divide the benefit, and the turn of the one who has lived in it exclusively, as aforesaid, comes, the other cannot count, against his turn, the time for which he occupied it before the division of the benefit, and prevent him from possessing it during his turn.

Time of occupation before division cannot be taken into account.

ART. 237.—In order that the division of the benefits may be irrevocable, it is required that the consent of the Mutevelli should be given.

Therefore a partition of the benefits agreed between the joint owners by mutual consent, without the leave of the Mutevelli, is not irrevocable, that is to say, whichever of the joint owners wishes can annul this division of the benefit at his will, without the consent of the other joint owner.

Division of benefit not irrevocable unless trustee consents.

ART. 238.—The separation of Ijaretein vaqf properties is allowed.

That is to say, one can separate part of an Ijaretein vaqf property and keep it in his possession and grant the rest to another.

The validity of the separation depends on the existence of the two conditions following :—

(*a*) the possibility of enjoying separately the benefit of each part separated.

(*b*) the fact that the separation is more beneficial to the dedication.

And in separation also the leave of the Mutevelli is required. Consequently, a separation made without the leave of the Mutevelli is invalid and of no force.

Power to alienate part.

ART. 239.—When a joint owner refuses to take, at its equivalent Muajele, a Mahlul share in an Ijaretein vaqf property, and at the same time does not ask to take it in common with the other owners for the assessed Muajele, and if the grant to another is beneficial to the dedication, and the unowned part can be separated, or is separated, in such a case the Mutevelli can separate the unowned part and grant it to another for the equivalent Muajele.

Grant of unowned part by Mutevelli.

SECTION X.

Certain questions relating to Ijaretein vaqf properties possessed in common.

ART. 240.—If two persons have joint and undivided possession of Ijaretein vaqf property, one cannot compel the other to grant him his share in the property or to take from him his own share in the property.

Alienation by joint owners.

But whichever of them wishes can grant his share to anyone he likes.

The grant made by one joint owner cannot be prevented.

The same rule is applied when there are more than two joint owners.

No pre-emption by Sacred Law. ART. 241.—In respect of Ijaretein vaqf properties, there is no right of pre-emption.

Consequently, one joint owner of Ijaretein vaqf properties can grant his share to another person without the permission of the other joint owner.

After the grant, the other joint owner cannot, on payment to the grantee of the price which he has paid, take that share, without the consent of the grantee, on the ground that he is joint owner of the property.

Again if two possess in common and in undivided shares an Ijaretein vaqf property, and one of them dies, leaving no one having the right to inherit, and the Mutevelli grant his share, which became Mahlul by his death to another for the Muajele assessed, the other co-owners cannot, on payment of the said Muajele to the person who took that share, take the share from him without his consent.

Right of pre-emption over unowned share by Civil Law. By the Civil Law however it is required with reference to Ijaretein vaqf dwellings and houses, which belong to the sort which does not produce income, that they should not be granted to another when a co-owner seeks an unowned share, and that there should be a reduction for the benefit of the co-owners.

No right of contribution for repairs. ART. 242.—If one of the co-owners of an Ijaretein vaqf property voluntarily repairs it at his own expense, he cannot seek from his co-owner a proportional part of the expense.

But if he repair it by the order of the co-owner under the condition that he should have a right of bringing it into account, then he can demand from him a sum proportional to his share.

Recovery of repair of ruined vaqf when made by order of judge. ART. 243.—If an Ijaretein vaqf property held in common which is not capable of division, or of which the division will cause damage to the dedication, is destroyed, and one of the co-owners wishes to repair it at his own expense, setting off the expense against the Muajele, but the rest do not agree to such repair, the co-owner, seeking to make the repair, applies to the judge, who, if the Mutevelli approve, gives him leave to repair that property, on condition that he repair it as aforesaid and take the part of the expenses, falling proportionally on the co-owners, out of the rent of that property.

The co-owner having repaired as aforesaid that property and having expended a reasonable sum out of his own estate, after leave given, lets that property and takes the rent, until he has received a sum equal to the amount of the expenses, which should be paid by the other co-owners.

SECTION XI.

Feragh bil vefa (Art. 19) and istiglal (Art. 20).

ART. 244.—The owner of an Ijaretein vaqf property can sell it, with power of redemption, for a debt due from him (*see* Mejellé, Art. 396). *Sale with power of redemption.*

For such a sale the leave of the Mutevelli is required, and if it is made without the leave of the Mutevelli it has no validity or force.

ART. 245.—Feragh bil vefa, or istiglal of an undivided part of an Ijaretein property is allowed, whether the property is susceptible of division or no. *Mortgage of part.*

Consequently, a man is allowed to grant to his creditor by feragh bil vefa or istiglal, a known undivided part, such as a half or a third of an Ijaretein property.

Also it is allowed for one to grant to his creditor, by feragh bil vefa or istiglal, his undivided share in a property which he possesses in Ijaretein in common with another.

ART. 246.—A person, who has let his Ijaretein vaqf property to another and given possession, may grant it to his creditor by feragh bil vefa by leave of the Mutevelli. *Mortgage of leased property.*

ART. 247.—When one pays his debt to the person who took his property by feragh bil vefa, he takes back the property from the grantee, the grant being annulled by leave of the Mutevelli. *On payment grant annulled by leave of Mutevelli.*

If the grantor, before his debt is paid to the grantee, dies leaving heirs entitled to inherit, the grantee can retain and hold the property until he receives his debt. *Mortgagee can hold against heir until payment.*

Consequently, the heirs, having the right to inherit, cannot interfere with the property granted, before the debt of the deceased is paid to the grantee.

ART. 248.—If the grantor, leaving no one entitled to inherit, die before he has paid his debt to the grantee, his debt is not secured by the property granted. The property belonging as Mahlul to the vaqf (23 Ramazan, 1286). *Where property becomes Mahlul, the security ceases.*

But if the property granted is a lawful (nizamli) vaqf ghedik held in Ijaretein, or vaqf Mussaqafat or Mustaghelat, in respect of which the extension of the right of inheritance has been effected according to the law, then, if the grantor die, leaving no one entitled to inherit, and there is not sufficient estate to pay his debt, the person who has taken by feragh bil vefa, when the property has been let by the vaqf for a rent payable in advance (Muajele) and possession delivered, may take out of this rent payable in advance (Muajele) the sum he is entitled to claim from the deceased. *When debt payable out of the Muajele.*

G

ART. 249.—If Ijaretein mussaqafat mevquf granted by feragh bil vefa or istiglal are burnt in a conflagration, the debt of the grantee is not extinguished, even if he was in possession.

In such a case the grantee can demand his debt from the grantor (*compare* Mejellé, 399).

ART. 250.—If someone grant his Ijaretein vaqf property to his creditor for his debt, subject to a power of redemption, and say that the sale shall be changed into a final sale if he do not pay the debt within a fixed time, and afterwards, when the time passes, the grantor cannot pay the debt, in such a case that grant is not considered to be turned into a final grant by reason only of what was said by the grantor.

In such a case, the grantor, if he pays his debt to the grantee, can take back from him that property if the Mutevelli think fit.

ART. 251.—The deferred rent (Muejele) for Ijaretein vaqf property, granted, subject to a power of redemption, to a creditor, is payable, as before, by the grantor and not by the grantee.

The same rule applies to grants by istiglal.

ART. 252.—The benefits of Ijaretein vaqf property, granted by feragh bil vefa, belong to the grantor and not to the grantee.

Consequently, if one grant to his creditor his Ijaretein vaqf property by feragh bil vefa, he can let the property to another, taking the rent for himself.

The person taking the property by feragh bil vefa, has no right to interfere in respect of the rent.

ART. 253.—By the death of the person, to whom an estate is granted by feragh bil vefa, the property granted does not become ownerless (Mahlul).

That is to say, if someone has, with the leave of the Mutevelli, conveyed his Ijaretein vaqf property to his creditor by feragh bil vefa, and afterwards the creditor dies without children, the property does not become Mahlul.

But if the grantor pays his debt to the heirs of the deceased creditor, he rescinds, if the Mutevelli approve, the grant by feragh bil vefa and possesses that property as before.

The grant by istiglal is similar to the grant by feragh bil vefa.

ART. 254.—The lease of Ijaretein vaqf property, granted by istiglal, made by the grantee to the grantor, is not valid unless the property has been previously quitted by the grantor and delivered to the grantee.

Consequently, the letting of the property is invalid if the grantee let it to the grantor before the quitting and delivery has been effected as above-mentioned.

In such a case, if the grantee by virtue of such letting receive any money as rent from the grantor, the grantee can set this sum off against the debt of the grantor.

N.B. As to powers of sale in mortgages, see Art. 261.

SECTION XII.

Questions relating to a mandate to make and a mandate to accept a grant.

ART. 255.—A person who has a mandate to sell Ijaretein vaqf property cannot sell it at a price excessively less than its equivalent value (*compare* Mejellé, Art. 1494). *Agent cannot sell for excessively low price.*

If he do so, the grant of the property is subject to the approval of the person who gave the mandate.

Consequently, if the person who gave the mandate approves of the sale, it is valid.

In case the mandator reject the grant, it is invalid, and the mandator takes back the property granted from the grantee with the approval of the Mutevelli.

ART. 256.—A mandatary to convey Ijaretein vaqf property cannot take the property for himself. *Agent to sell cannot buy.*

ART. 257.—A mandatary to convey Ijaretein vaqf property cannot grant it to persons whose evidence is not admissible on his behalf, such as his children, parents and wife. *Agent to sell cannot sell to his relations.*

But if the mandator appoint a mandatary to convey the property to one of those persons, or make general the mandate by saying, " grant it to whomsoever you wish," in such a case the mandatary can convey the property to such relations of his (*see* Mejellé, Art. 1497).

ART. 258.—If a mandatary to accept a grant of Ijaretein vaqf property, no price being fixed by the mandator, take the property for the mandator at a price excessively above its equivalent value, the conveyance is not to be carried out as regards the mandator. *Agent cannot buy for an excessively high price.*

ART. 259.—In case of dismissal by the act of the mandator, it is required that the mandatary should have knowledge of the dismissal (Mejellé, Art. 1523). *Revocation of authority by principal notice necessary.*

Consequently, if the mandator dismiss a mandatary appointed to sell Ijaretein vaqf property, and the latter sell the property with the leave of the Mutevelli before notice of his dismissal has reached him, the sale is valid and of force.

But if he grant it after notice of his dismissal has reached him, the sale has no force or validity.

ART. 260.—In the case of dismissal by act of law, that is to say where it arises in consequence of the death of the mandator, it is not required that the mandatary should have knowledge of it (*see* Mejellé, Art. 1527).

Consequently, if the mandator die before the mandatary grant the Ijaretein vaqf property, which he has a mandate to grant, and afterwards the mandatary grant it to another, in every case the grant has no force and is not to be carried out, whether at the time of the grant notice of the death of the mandator had reached the mandatary or not.

In such a case, if the mandator has left heirs with the right to inherit, they can disapprove of the grant and take back the property from the grantee, by virtue of their succession to the property alone.

If the grantor leave no heirs having the right to inherit, that property belongs to the vaqf as Mahlul, and the grantee takes back the price if he has paid it.

Mandate to sell
for benefit of
creditor.

ART. 261.—When a man grants his Ijaretein vaqf property to his creditor by feragh bil vefa, and gives a mandate to the creditor to sell the property at its equivalent value and take his debt out of the price, if he cannot pay the debt within a fixed period, and the debtor cannot pay his debt within the time fixed, the creditor by virtue of the mandate can convey the property, so mortgaged, to another and take his debt out of the price (Mejellé, Art. 760).

Again, when one grants to his creditor Ijaretein vaqf property by feragh bil vefa, if he give a mandate to a third person to sell this property for its equivalent value, and pay his creditor out of the price in case he cannot discharge his debt within a fixed time, and he is not able to discharge his debt at the expiration of the time fixed. In such a case the mandatary sells this property for its equivalent value, pays the debt out of the price, and returns to the mandator any surplus which may remain after payment of the debt.

In such a case, if, at the expiration of the period, the mandatary refuses to sell the property and pay the debt, the judge orders him to execute the transfer and pay the debt.

ART. 262.—If someone has appointed another his mandatary to purchase a specified Ijaretein vaqf property for a certain price, and the mandatary purchase that property for himself for the said price, and take out a title deed in his own name, by the permission of the Mutevelli, the mandator can, with the approval of the Mutevelli, take that property from the mandatary, cause the title deed to be set aside, and take a title deed in his own name (*see* Mejellé, Arts. 1485, 1486).

SECTION XIII.
Miscellaneous questions.

ART. 263.—The possessor of Ijaretein vaqf property is the owner of the benefits derived from the property, but is not the owner of its reqabe. *(Trustee can recover for waste.)*

Consequently, if one pulls down a building on a Mussaqafat Ijaretein vaqf property and sell and deliver the materials to another, and consume them, the Mutevelli demands and recovers from him, as damages, the worth of the property as it stood.

ART. 264.—When the possessor of Ijaretein vaqf property lets it to another and puts him in possession, and goes to another country, the jabi vaqf (collector of the rents of the vaqf) has no right to demand from the lessee the Muejele which is in arrear. *(Lessee not liable for Muejele.)*

ART. 265.—When it is published that the possessor of Ijaretein vaqf property has died in a foreign country where he has gone, and the Mutevelli, there being no person who has a right to inherit, thinking that the property has become Mahlul, grants it to another for an equivalent Muajele if afterwards the possessor, being alive, appears, he takes from the grantee the property, and the grantee takes back from the Mutevelli the Muajele. *(Grant of property as Mahlul by mistake.)*

But he, whose death was given out, can approve of the grant made by the Mutevelli and take from the Mutevelli for himself the Muajele.

ART. 266.—If, when the possessor of Ijaretein vaqf property dies, the Mutevelli, thinking that he has left no heirs to inherit, grant the property to another and afterwards heirs of the dead man, having a right to inherit, appear, the provisions of the preceding article are applied.

ART. 267.—It is not allowed to change the ancient state of Mussaqafat vaqf. *(Change of condition of roofed vaqfs by permission of judge.)*

But when the necessity for a change, and, that it will be beneficial to the vaqf, is shewn, then a change is allowed with the approval of the judge and the permission of the Mutevelli.

E.g. When there is an Ijaretein vaqf bath, and it is shewn that on account of its size it costs a large expenditure to warm it, and benefit is not derived from it, because the inhabitants in the neighbourhood are few, and it is shewn that if it is preserved in its existing state it will remain useless, and from this the dedication will sustain great loss, and it is at the same time shewn that the separation of a part of the bath and the building on that part of another small bath, and on the remaining portion, a property such as a workshop or inn on account of the vaqf will be beneficial to the vaqf; if the Mutevelli with the approval of the judge give leave to the possessor of the said bath, to build in the manner above stated, this permission is lawful and of force.

Building on Ijaretein vaqf land.

ART. 268.—If the owner of an Ijaretein vaqf site wish to erect a building on it, with the intention that it shall be his own property, the Mutevelli can prevent him.

In such a case, if the possessor without the leave of the Mutevelli, erect a building on the site, in order that it may be his own property, the following rules are observed:

If the pulling down of that building will not damage the site, it is pulled down.

If the pulling down is hurtful, the value of the building and materials is given to the person who built it, from the vaqf, and by his consent it is bought for the vaqf.

In such a case, the Mutevelli of that site, cannot contend that that building is the property of the vaqf by reason only that in the title deed of the land a condition is inserted that whatever the possessor builds on it should be given to the vaqf.

Muajele is income not corpus.

ART. 269.—The rent taken from the lessee, on account of the vaqf, under the name " Muajele," at the granting of the lease, is not considered as belonging to the corpus but to the income of the vaqf.

Therefore, the Muajele is expended for the needs of the dedication in accordance with the direction of the dedicator.

CHAPTER VII.
Ijare-i-vahide vaqf immovable properties.

Vahide vaqfs. what they are.

ART. 270.—Ijare-i-vahide vaqfs are those let by their Mutevellis, at a rack rent, to those who propose to take them for a time, such as a month or a year, the rents being expended for the purposes appointed by the dedicator.

In such vahide vaqfs, the rules, such as those which deal with the possession for life and transmission to the children have no force, but immediately on the expiration of the term of the letting, the Mutevelli of the vaqf can let them to another.

The term for which the Mutevelli may let.

ART. 271.—It is necessary to observe the condition, which the dedicator should have imposed, about the term for which the vahide vaqf may be let.

E.g. If the dedicator impose a condition that the property which he dedicated is to be let for eight or five years, the letting is to be carried out in accordance with this condition.

ART. 272.—If the dedicator has not made mention of any condition about the time of letting, if the thing let is a chiftlik, or lands, it cannot be let for more than three years, or if it be other property, for more than one year. ^{Where the dedicator has given no directions.}

But when by a lease for a longer term than the said periods, there arises benefit and use to the dedication, the letting of the dedicated property for a longer period may be allowed with the consent of the judge (Law 10 Rebiul Evvel, 1291, Art. 165).

ART. 273.—When the Mutevelli of the dedication has let and delivered a vahide vaqf until the completion of the period fixed, and after the expiration of the term of the lease, having received the property from the lessee, wishes to let it to another, the lessee cannot oppose the Mutevelli and refuse to deliver up that property on the ground that he has a prior right over the other to a lease, and that if he offers the same rent it ought to be let again to him. ^{Lessee has no right to renewal.}

ART. 274.—The Mutevelli cannot let and deliver a vahide vaqf property at a Muqata'a (Art. 39) rent. If he does so, the letting is not valid and of force. ^{As to letting vahidele at Muqata'a rent.}

But when the building of a vahide Mussaqafat vaqf is burnt or falls into decay and thus a bare building site remains, if there is no one willing to rent it at a vahide rent, on the condition that he shall set off the expenses against the rent, and there is not sufficient income from the dedicated property to rebuild, in such a case the Mutevelli can let the land at a Muqata'a rent.

This must be done by the permission of the judge and the leave of the Sultan.

Consequently, if the Mutevelli let that land at a Muqata'a rent of his own motion and without the permission of the judge and the leave of the Sultan, the lease is of no force or validity.

ART. 275.—The Mutevelli cannot, contrary to the condition of the dedicator, let property as Ijaretein which has been dedicated under the condition that it shall be let at a vahide rent. ^{When vahidele may be let as Ijareteinle (Art. 37).}

But in case Mussaqafat vaqf property, directed to be let at a vahide rent, falls down, and the property of the dedication has not sufficient income to repair it, and no one can be found to rent it at a vahide rent and repair it, setting off the expenses against the rent, then the Mutevelli may, with the approval of the judge and the permission of the Sultan, let that Mussaqafat as Ijaretein.

But if the Mutevelli of his own motion let it as Ijaretein without the decision of the judge and the leave of the Sultan, such letting has no force or validity.

If the Mutevelli letting it of his own motion as Ijaretein deliver to the lessee a title to say that he possesses it as such, then that title has no force and is not to be given effect to.

The other laws and questions relating to vahide vaqfs are set out in the chapter about letting vaqfs (*see* Arts. 165, 383, 401 and note).

CHAPTER VIII.

The Laws relating to Muqata'alu vaqfs.

In Muqata'alu lands are vaqf houses, etc., mulk.

ART. 276.—The land of vaqfs let at Muqa'ata rent is vaqf, but buildings on them or trees or vines are the pure mulk property of the person possessing them.

Sometimes houses, etc., are dedicated separately.

Sometimes, however, when these buildings or trees or vines are dedicated by their owner to a vaqf, the land is attached to one vaqf, and the buildings, trees or vines upon it to another, so therefore the Muqata'a rent ought to be given by the vaqf in favour of which the buildings, trees or vines are dedicated, to the vaqf in whose favour the land is dedicated.

Land subject to building etc.

ART. 277.—The land of vaqfs let at a Muqata'a rent is subject to the buildings, trees or vines upon it.

Consequently, into whosoever's ownership the buildings, trees or vines may come, the vaqf land in subjection to them comes also into his possession.

E.g. If someone sell to another a house, of which the site is Muqata'alu vaqf and the buildings pure mulk, or trees of which the site is Muqata'alu vaqf but the trees mulk, or vines of which the site is Muqata'alu vaqf but the vines are mulk, the site also comes into the possession of the buyer.

Consequently, there is no necessity for a special grant of the site with the permission of the Mutevelli of the vaqf.

House, etc., may be sold and site kept.

However if the seller declare clearly at the time of the sale that he keeps possession of the site, the site does not come into the possession of the purchaser.

Land may be sold and house, etc., kept.

But if he grant, by leave of the Mutevelli, the land to another, he does not include in the sale the mulk property upon it, buildings, trees or vines, since he grants only the site, it is not considered that he has sold to the person, to whom he made the grant, the buildings, trees and vines upon it.

When owner dies, the land follows the buildings.

Again, when the owner of mulk buildings, trees or vines, situated on a Muqata'alu vaqf site dies and either the persons entitled to a share of his property or the heirs in the male and female line inherit the buildings, trees or vines, the land also comes into the possession of the said heirs gratis, without payment, as subject to the buildings, trees and vines.

ART. 278.—When one is owner of buildings on a Muqata'alu vaqf site and of trees and vines planted on it, and possesses the site at a Muqata'a rent, and dies without children, and his heirs wish to take the buildings, trees and vines by virtue of their right of inheritance, and the site as subject to them, without payment, the Mutevelli cannot prevent the heirs occupying it, on the ground that, since the site is vaqf, the buildings, trees and vines on it also belong to the dedication.

When owner dies, buildings, etc., do not belong to the dedication.

ART. 279.—When one possesses Muqata'alu vaqf which has no buildings, trees or vines upon it, and grants it to another, in order that the grant may be valid the leave of the Mutevelli is required.

Leave of Mutevelli required for grant of site.

Consequently, in such a case, if he grant the site without the leave of the Mutevelli, the grant has no force or validity.

Whence if one possesses the Muqata'alu vaqf site of a property, and another owns the buildings, trees or vines, when the person in possession grants that site, he must obtain the leave of the Mutevelli.

In the same way, if there are mulk buildings, trees or vines on a Muqata'alu site, but their owner grants only the site, not selling the buildings, trees or vines, in order that the grant may be valid, the leave of the Mutevelli is required.

ART. 280.—If one wish to give to another the buildings, trees and vines of an estate of which the land is Muqata'alu vaqf, but the appurtenances, such as the house, workshop, vineyard and garden are mulk, in order that the gift may be valid, it is necessary that before the gift, the site should be granted to the donee, by leave of the Mutevelli.

Gift of mulk property on Muqata'alu.

Consequently the gift is not valid, unless the grant of the site of the mulk property is made to the donee, with the leave of the Mutevelli.

Nevertheless, however, where the donee is an infant, and the donor is his guardian, then it is not necessary that the site should be granted in order that the gift may be valid.

ART. 281.—When joint owners divide the buildings, trees and vines, being mulk, but situated on a Muqata'alu vaqf site, then the site also is considered as divided, in subjection to them.

Partition of Muqata'alu vaqfs.

Consequently, the division does not require the leave of the Mutevelli in order that it may be valid.

But if Muqata'alu vaqf land, having no buildings, trees or vines upon it, is divided between the joint owners, then the leave of the Mutevelli is required.

ART. 282.—As long as there are traces of buildings, trees or vines on a Muqata'alu vaqf site, the owner of the buildings, trees or vines keeps possession of the site.

But if, when no traces of buildings, trees or vines exist, the possessor of the site does not re-erect buildings, or plant anew trees or vines, and does not pay to the vaqf the original Muqata'a rent, then the Mutevelli puts a stop to the rent, takes the site out of the hands of the person who possesses it and grants it to another.

But as long as the person who possesses the site duly pays the rent at the right time, the Mutevelli cannot cancel this rent and take the site out of the hands of the possessor, even if no trace of buildings, trees or vines remain.

ART. 283.—If the Muqata'a rent originally fixed in respect of a property of which the site is Muqata'alu vaqf but the buildings, trees or vines mulk, is below the rent of the site valued according to the time and the condition of the property, this rent is raised so as to be equal to the rent at a valuation (*see* also 3 Zilkade, 1295, after the occupation of Cyprus).

ART. 284.—Since the buildings, trees and vines situated on a Muqata'alu vaqf site are looked upon as moveables, with regard to them the regulations about moveables are of force.

Consequently, in respect of these, no right of pre-emption exists, that is to say, these things cannot be property over which a person has a right of pre-emption, or property by virtue of the possession of which a person has a right of pre-emption (*see* Mejellé, 952, 953 and 1008).

ART. 285.—If a person, possessing at a Muqata'a rent, a plot of land out of real vaqf lands, which has no buildings, trees or vines upon it, dies, that piece of land passes by inheritance in equal shares to the sons and daughters only of the dead man and not to his other heirs.

But if the Muqata'alu vaqf plot is of the unreal vaqfs which are of the Takhsisat category, then, since, in regard to it, the rules of the law of Arazi mirié is applied, it passes, like Arazi mirié to eight degrees of relations.

ART. 286.—When a place dedicated originally as Ijaretein is converted into a public establishment, such as a hospital and school, whether by Ottoman subjects or foreigners, then that place ought with the consent of the Mutevelli and the permission of the Sultan to be turned into Muqata'alu vaqf (as to compensation to the vaqf 16 Ramazan, 1299, after the occupation of Cyprus; *see* also note).

CHAPTER IX.
Matters relating to the Office of the Mutevelli.
SECTION I.
Appointment of the Mutevelli.

ART. 287.—The Mutevelli must be of sound mind, of age, trustworthy and able to direct the affairs of the vaqf.

Consequently, a person who combines all these qualities can be appointed Mutevelli.

Who may be Mutevelli.

ART. 288.—If the person, in whose favour the office of Mutevelli is created, is a minor, a substitute is appointed by the judge to manage the affairs of the Mutevelliship until the Mutevelli is of age and able to direct them.

When afterwards the minor becomes of age and competent to discharge the duties of the Mutevelliship, he takes upon himself its direction, and the substitute is withdrawn.

Substitute during minority. Qaimaqam-i-Mutevelli, Art. 10.

ART. 289.—It is not required that the Mutevelli should be a male. Therefore a woman can be Mutevelli.

A woman may be Mutevelli.

ART. 290.—One and the same person can be Mutevelli of many vaqfs. So also many persons can be Mutevelli of one vaqf.

Pluralities—joint Mutevellis.

ART. 291.—The office of Mutevelli is not given to the person applying for it. Unless the Mutevelliship was appointed to him by the dedicator, in that case it is given to him.

Appointee of dedicator alone can demand Mutevelliship.

ART. 292.—When the Mutevelli of a vaqf dies or is dismissed, it is required that a Mutevelli be immediately appointed by the judge, in order that the affairs of the vaqf may not remain without direction.

The judge cannot refuse to appoint a Mutevelli until the accounts of the preceding Mutevelli have been examined.

On cessation, judge to appoint new Mutevelli.

ART. 293.—The dedicator himself directs the affairs of a vaqf of which the Mutevelliship is not appointed in favour of anyone.

When the dedicator dies, the office of Mutevelli must be conferred by the judge.

Consequently, the children of the dedicator, even if there are any capable of acting, cannot of their own will without an appointment by the judge, become Mutevellis of a vaqf of which no Mutevelli has been appointed.

But the vacant office of Mutevelli not appointed to anyone as above stated, is given to the children and family of the dedicator in preference to strangers.

Consequently, when there are children and relations capable of directing the business of the Mutevelliship and entitled to it, the judge cannot grant it to a stranger.

If no Mutevelli appointed, dedicator is Mutevelli for life.

After death of dedicator, a Mutevelli is appointed by judge.

Family of dedicator preferred.

If he do so, the Mutevelliship is given to one of the children or family, and the stranger is dispensed with.

But by law. it is not allowed to interfere with the management of the Mutevelliship which is appointed by the dedicator to a stranger, and give it to one of the children or family of the dedicator (*see* Art. 165).

Mutevelli appointed to obtain judicial sanction (*see* Arts. 111 and 121).

ART. 294.—The duties of the Mutevelli, appointed by the dedicator to obtain the judicial declaration of irrevocability alone terminate from the time of the completion of that declaration.

Consequently, that Mutevelli has no authority, after the judicial decision has been given, to mix himself up in the affairs of the Mutevelliship.

E.g. Suppose one dedicates certain things, and, having obtained the judicial decision, die after he has directed for some time the affairs of the dedication, without appointing the Mutevelliship in favour of anyone, in such a case, the Mutevelli previously appointed by the dedicator for the purposes of the judicial decision cannot, solely on the ground that he was so appointed, contend that he is Mutevelli of that vaqf and dispute the lawfulness of the appointment of the Mutevelli appointed to that vaqf by the judge.

Mutevelli of one foundation not *ipso facto* Mutevelli of another made by the same dedicator.

ART. 295.—When someone, after he has dedicated a property and appointed a Mutevelli to it founds another vaqf and does not appoint a Mutevelli to it, the Mutevelli appointed for the administration of the first vaqf is not looked upon as the Mutevelli of the second vaqf by reason only of his appointment fo the first vaqf.

As regards the Mutevelliship of the second vaqf, the rules contained in the preceding article are complied with.

If no Mutevelli is appointed, executor of dedicator is Mutevelli.

ART. 296.—If someone, not having appointed a Mutevelli to a vaqf which he has consecrated, die leaving a will in force by which he had appointed a guardian for the execution of the will, this guardian is looked upon as Mutevelli of the dedication.

Appointment obtained by false representation is invalid.

ART. 297.—The grant of the Mutevelliship made on a false representation is not valid, even if the grant of a Berat has been obtained.

E.g. If, while there are children of the testator living, in favour of whom it is directed that they should manage the affairs of the Mutevelliship, the person in whose favour the Mutevelliship is appointed on failure of the children of the testator, by means of untrue representations, obtain his own appointment by the judge to the Mutevelliship, his appointment is invalid and of no force.

Again, the appointment of a Mutevelli is invalid, if he asserts before the judge, contrary to the truth, that the office of Mutevelli to a vaqf is vacant, and so is appointed Mutevelli while a Mutevelli exists and is alive.

ART. 298.—In the case of a Mutevelliship granted to the most competent of the children of the dedicator, the son or daughter who is most competent acquires the right and it is limited in favour of him or her.

If several of the children of the dedicator claim the Mutevelliship, each seeking that it should be granted to him, it is granted to the one shewing himself to be the most competent; when it is shewn that some of the children of the dedicator are equal as regards competency, it is granted to them equally.

Males are not preferred to females.

ART. 299.—If the office of Mutevelli, limited in favour of the elder child of the dedicator, is vacant, and there are two elder children of the same age, the office is given to the one best acquainted with the affairs of the dedication.

If both have the same knowledge, the Mutevelliship is given equally to both.

ART. 300.—It is not allowed for one and the same person to be Mutevelli and overseer (Nazir vaqf).

Consequently, if the Mutevelli of a vaqf is appointed also to the overseership (Nazaret) or the overseer to the Mutevelliship and the Berat is given, he is removed from the Mutevelliship or overseership, as the case may be and it is given to the person who has a right to it.

ART. 301.—If the person to fill a vacant Mutevelliship is defined so that there is no difficulty in knowing him, he becomes Mutevelli of the vaqf without being appointed by the judge.

E.g. If the Mutevelliship of a vaqf situated in Constantinople, is limited in favour of the person holding the office of Fetva Emini (keeper of fetvas), the latter is Mutevelli of that vaqf without any judicial appointment and he manages its affairs.

Again, when the Mutevelliship of a vaqf limited in favour of the elder son of the dedicator becomes vacant, the elder in age becomes Mutevelli without judicial appointment.

But if the person to be Mutevelli is not defined so as to be easily known, the appointment of the Mutevelli depends on the decision of the judge.

E.g. If the vacant post is given to the most competent of the children of the dedicator, and there are several of them, each asserting that he is the most competent, none of them can take up the duties of the Mutevelliship, until, first, it has been shewn, in the way required by law, that he is the most competent, and his appointment has been decided on by the judge.

When
Mutevelli
called
Inspector (see
Art. 11.)

ART. 302.—If a dedicator, who dwells in a city, where the word "inspectorship (Nazaret)," is customarily used instead of "Mutevelliship" appoint for his dedicated property a Nazir alone, he is also looked upon as Mutevelli. There is no necessity for the appointment of another.

SECTION II.

Appointment of a Qaimaqam-i-Mutevelli and the grant of the Mutevelliship by the Mutevelli.

When judge
can appoint a
person to act
as Mutevelli.

ART. 303.—The judge cannot appoint a Qaimaqam-i-Mutevelli to a vaqf, which has its Mutevelli, where there is no necessity for it.

If he does so, the appointment has no validity or force. That is to say, the management of the affairs of the vaqf by the substitute appointed, is not executory or of force.

When, however, there is necessity for it, the judge can appoint a Qaimaqam-i-Mutevelli.

E.g. The judge appoints temporarily a Qaimaqam-i-Mutevelli to carry on the affairs of the dedication in order to prevent their remaining unexecuted, if, after the Mutevelli has been looked for, he cannot be found, or if without appointing someone with the necessary powers, he has gone away to another city situated a long distance away, or if the Mutevelli appointed by the dedicator is a minor (*see* note).

Again if, although there is a Mutevelli of a vaqf the appointment of a Qaimaqam is required for a law suit, or some act requiring a Qaimaqam, then a Qaimaqam is is appointed by the judge.

E.g. If those possessing two adjacent Ijaretein properties, each of which depends on its own dedication, bring a lawsuit against each other and the Mutevelli of the two vaqfs is one and the same person, then the judge appoints a Qaimaqam-i-Mutevelli to one of the vaqfs for the purposes of the lawsuit.

Again, if when the office of Mutevelli appointed by the dedicator is vacant before the person in whose favour the Mutevelliship is limited is determined, the reare persons who assert that each of them is the appointed Mutevelli, the judge appoints a Qaimaqam-i-Mutevelli until the end of the lawsuit, that he may be useful to him as a suitor, and he hears the action of the contending parties in his presence and gives judgment.

Whenever a Mutevelli is accused of bad faith or abuse of trust, a Qaimaqam is appointed by the judge to bring an action against the Mutevelli.

Again if a person possessing an Ijaretein vaqf property is appointed Mutevelli of that vaqf, and afterwards wishes to grant that property to another, or if a Mutevelli out of the estate, of which he is Mutevelli, wishes to take an Ija-retein vaqf from the person who possesses it for the equivalent value, a Mutevelli can be appointed to give permission for the transfer.

Also if a Mutevelli of dedicated money, who wishes to borrow money out of it, applies to the judge, the judge appoints temporarily a Qaimaqam-i-Mutevelli to that vaqf in order that he may lend to the Mutevelli.

ART. 304.—If it is shewn that a Mutevelli, although he is honest, is unable to manage the affairs of the vaqf, the judge can appoint a Qaimaqam to help him.

Incapable Mutevelli.

ART. 305.—In the above articles, the judge is required to have authority from the Sultan to appoint Qaimaqam-i-Mutevellis.

Judge must have authority from the Sultan.

Consequently, a judge who has no authority from the Sultan to appoint Qaimaqam-i-Mutevellis, cannot appoint a Mutevelli. If he do so, the appointment is invalid and of no force.

ART. 306.—The Mutevelli appointed by the dedicator can grant his Mutevelliship to another during the time of his administration.

Grant of office to another, (see Art. 376, 380.)

But this grant is not an irrevocable agreement, but a commission given by the Mutevelli to another for the discharge of the Mutevelli's duties. For this reason, the grantor can revoke his grant when he wishes.

When the grantor dies, the grant, being looked upon as a commission, ceases to have any force.

The Mutevelliship belongs to the person in whose favour it is limited.

The person, to whom the grant was made, has no longer any right as regards the management of the affairs of the vaqf.

These rules also are complied with in respect of other posts appointed by the dedicator.

ART. 307.—If a person occupying a Mutevelli's post, not limited by the dedicator in favour of anyone, grant it to another in the presence of the judge, and the judge, by the reason of his fitness shewn, bestow the Mutevelliship on the person in whose favour the grant is made, the grantor can no longer revoke the grant.

Irrevocable grant.

SECTION III.

Questions relating to the accounts of the Mutevelli.

ART. 308.—When there is a Mutevelli of a vaqf, the judge cannot interfere in the management of that vaqf.

Right of judge to examine accounts.

But the judges are entitled to watch over and examine the vaqf properties.

That is to say, when the judge from certain evidence suspects bad faith or abuse of trust by the Mutevelli, he immediately examines the acts of the Mutevelli in respect of the vaqf and looks into his accounts.

Dismissal of Mutevelli for bad faith.

If at the examination, bad faith calling for the dismissal of the Mutevelli is shewn, the judge dismisses him, even if he be the dedicator himself.

Mutevelli must submit his accounts to the judge.

ART. 309.—The Mutevelli cannot refuse to submit his accounts to the judge, when, in case of need, he wishes to see them.

If he refuses, he is compelled to submit his accounts.

Re-opening accounts.

ART. 310.—The accounts of any years of a Mutevelli which have been examined, cannot be re-examined if there is no cause at all for suspicion. But if there is any suspicion in the matter of the accounts, the Mutevelli is interrogated and in case of necessity the accounts are again examined to clear away the suspicion.

Accounts of preceding Mutevelli.

ART. 311.—When the Mutevelli of a vaqf submits his accounts for the time of his administration, the judge, if he is not satisfied with them, cannot demand from the Mutevelli the accounts of the preceding Mutevelli.

If the preceding Mutevelli is alive, the accounts must be gone into with him himself. If he is dead, with his heirs. The successor is not responsible for the accounts of his predecessor.

Where dedicator directs that the accounts are to be examined, if the officials think fit, judge cannot examine of his own motion.

ART. 312.—If the dedicator direct that the accounts of the Mutevelli are to be examined, if the vaqf officials think fit, the judge cannot of his own motion, without taking the opinion of the officials, look into the accounts of the Mutevelli. If he do so, it has no effect, and the accounts of the Mutevelli are again examined if the officials think fit.

SECTION IV.

For what causes a Mutevelli may be dismissed.

No dismissal without fault (see Art. 373).

ART. 313.—A Mutevelli, who has committed no fault, and who is legally appointed, cannot be dismissed even by the judge who appointed him. If the judge do so, the Mutevelli is not considered as dismissed.

Dismissal for bad faith (see 330, 308).

Nevertheless when bad faith on the part of the Mutevelli, in the management of the vaqf, is proved according to law in his presence, he must be dismissed from the Mutevelliship even if he be the dedicator himself.

An act contrary to the Sacred Law is a breach of trust.

ART. 314.—It is looked upon as a breach of trust against the dedication if the Mutevelli proceed intentionally to an act relating to the management of the dedicated property which is not allowed by the Sacred Law.

E.g. It is looked upon as an act of bad faith against the vaqf, if the Mutevelli knowingly and without inevitable necessity let the property for a rent excessively less than the estimated rent, or if he sell the vaqf property to another as his own, or if he spend and lay out the income derived from the vaqf property on his own wants, contrary to the condition of the dedicator.

ART. 315.—It is considered a breach of trust on the part of the Mutevelli if he brings an action about the ownership of the property against the vaqf.

Unsuccessful action against the dedication.

That is to say, if the Mutevelli of a vaqf property brings an action, contending that certain property of that vaqf belongs to him, and he is not able to prove his contention, he is discharged from the Mutevelliship of that vaqf.

But if he proves his assertion he is not discharged from his Mutevelliship.

ART. 316.—The denial by the Mutevelli that property belongs to the vaqf is considered a breach of trust.

Wrongful claim to property of dedication.

That is to say, when an action is brought about a property found in the possession of the Mutevelli of a vaqf, on the ground that it belongs to the vaqf, if the Mutevelli declare that that property is his own private property, and denies the ownership of the vaqf, he is discharged from his Mutevelliship when it is legally proved and adjudged that that property belongs to the vaqf. If this is not shewn, he is not discharged from the Mutevelliship.

ART. 317.—Breach of trust is indivisible.

Mutevelli dismissed from one dedication is dismissed from all.

Consequently, when a breach of trust against one vaqf is legally proved against a Mutevelli, who is Mutevelli of many vaqfs, he is discharged from the Mutevelliship of all the vaqfs. He is not discharged from the Mutevelliship of that vaqf alone against which he is shewn to have been guilty of breach of trust.

ART. 318.—The Mutevelli is not discharged from the Mutevelliship, *ipso facto*, by the breach of trust and fault, but he is rendered liable to be dismissed.

Acts of Mutevelli before dismissal by judge are valid.

Consequently, if the Mutevelli perpetrate a breach of trust and fault against the vaqf, but, before he is dismissed by the judge, direct its affairs and effect during that time certain lawful acts of the vaqf, those acts are to be carried out and are of force.

ART. 319.—A Mutevelli is not discharged upon an accusation only.

Mutevelli not dismissed on mere accusation.

That is to say, if the officials and beneficiaries of a vaqf denounce the Mutevelli to the judge, but do not declare any lawful ground for his dismissal, or if they state that there is lawful ground for his dismissal but are not able to prove it, the judge cannot dismiss the Mutevelli, acting on the accusation alone.

H

Dismissal for depravity and extravagance.

ART. 320.—The Mutevelli's being given up to wickedness and extravagance results in his dismissal.

Consequently, even if breach of trust is not shewn, if the Mutevelli leads a life of depravity and extravagance the judge can dismiss him from his office.

Idleness and carelessness, (see Art. 381, 382).

ART. 321.—Idleness and carelessness of a Mutevelli in the affairs of the trust are cause for his dismissal.

Mental derangement.

ART. 322.—A Mutevelli is discharged from his office, who is struck by mental derangement lasting more than a year.

If in such a case, after he is discharged, he gets well, the following rules are observed :—

If he is a Mutevelli appointed by the dedicator, he takes up his duties again, otherwise not.

Blindness.

ART. 323.—The Mutevelli who becomes blind, is not discharged from his duties.

Mutevelli can resign.

ART. 324.—The Mutevelli can resign his office by himself.

But he is not discharged from his Mutevelliship until he has made known his renunciation to the judge or the dedicator.

Consequently, until his resignation is known to the judge or the dedicator, he preserves his office and his acts are to be carried out and are valid.

Re-instalment of depraved Mutevelli.

ART. 325.—After a Mutevelli has been dismissed for depravity and extravagance or for breach of trust, it is not allowed that the Mutevelliship should be given to him again before a long time has elapsed, and it is shewn that he is improved.

But when his improvement is shewn he can be appointed to the Mutevelliship.

CHAPTER X.

The duties, powers and rights of Mutevelli.

SECTION I.

Acts for which the Mutevelli is liable to make indemnity.

When he must consult judge.

ART. 326.—The Mutevelli transacts by himself the affairs which are within his jurisdiction and authority.

But he addresses himself to the judge for matters which are not within his jurisdiction and authority and of which the validity at law depends on the judge. If he manages such things by himself, his acts are of no force or validity (see Art. 275).

If more than one, all must consent.

ART. 327.—If there are two Mutevellis, one of them cannot transact business alone without the consent of the other.

If he do so and the other Mutevelli does not approve of the action and refuses to ratify it, the action is invalid.

The same rule applies when there are more than two Mutevellis.

ART. 328.—The Mutevelli cannot transact alone the affairs of the trust, if there is an overseer (Nazir) as well as a Mutevelli, unless he gets the consent of the overseer. If he do so, his action is not to be carried out.

Mutevelli must get the consent of the overseer.

ART. 329.—The Mutevelli is allowed in case of necessity to appoint an agent to transact the business of the trust.

Mutevelli may appoint agent.

Consequently, the Mutevelli is not liable to make good any loss which shall have resulted on account of his having appointed an agent to transact the affairs of the vaqf.

Because a man is not responsible for doing what is allowed by law (Mejellé, 91).

E.g. If the Mutevelli of a vaqf give a commission to a person, whom he thinks trustworthy, to collect from the debtors the amount due to the vaqf, and the agent collect the debts but spend what he collects on his own needs, the Mutevelli is not liable to make compensation.

But if the Mutevelli deposit and give the substance of the dedication to a person whom he does not trust and this person consume it, the Mutevelli must make compensation.

Liability of Mutevelli appointing improper agent.

ART. 330.—The Mutevelli of a vaqf, cannot by use of the property of the vaqf acquire Arazi mirié, or Arazi mevqufé, or an Ijaretein property in order that revenues from them may be obtained for the vaqf.

Mutevelli cannot acquire for the dedication Arazi mirié, etc.

If he do so, he is made to pay back the property of the dedication which he gave as the price for the thing acquired, and is liable to be dismissed (*see* Art. 314).

ART. 331.—The Mutevelli is bound to make compensation for any loss, which he has occasioned to the vaqf through his acting beyond the powers given by the vaqfieh, in a case in which the Sacred Law does not sanction it.

For acting beyond powers.

E.g. If a Mutevelli has dedicated money which the dedicator has directed to be let at interest on pledges or security by surety, and lets it without pledge or security and afterwards the debtor becomes bankrupt and the money cannot be recovered, the Mutevelli is bound to make indemnity.

Again, if the Mutevelli has money which the dedicator directed should be lent at interest on the security of a surety of credit :—That is to say a rich man—and contrary to the conditions lend it to another on the security of a surety unworthy of credit and afterwards cannot collect the money from the principal debtor or surety, he is liable to make good the loss.

But if at the time of the lending, the surety was worthy of credit and afterwards failed, then the Mutevelli is not liable to make good any loss.

Again, if a Mutevelli is authorized, by the conditions of the dedicator, to lend dedicated money on the security of a pledge greater in value than the loan, and take as security things of a less value, and the debtor die before he pay his debt, leaving no property except the things pledged. If when the pledge is sold the price is not sufficient to pay the debt, the Mutevelli makes good the loss by payment of the remainder of the debt.

But if at the time the loan is made, the value of the pledge is equal to the amount advanced and afterwards falls, then the Mutevelli is not bound to make good the loss.

In the same way if a Mutevelli lend dedicated money, which the dedicator has directed to be lent on a hujjet being drawn up, contrary to the direction of the dedicator, without applying to the Court, when the debt is not proved, and the debtor denies it on oath, and dedicated money is lost, the Mutevelli is liable to make good the loss.

So, if the Mutevelli keep money, which the dedicator has directed should be kept in a safe place, such as the bezestan, in his own house, and it is stolen therefrom, the Mutevelli is liable to make good the loss.

For expenditure not sanctioned by the dedicator.

ART. 332.—Expenses incurred by the Mutevelli not sanctioned by the conditions imposed by the dedicator are not allowed.

E.g. If grants from the income of a true Mustaghelat vaqf, contrary to the conditions of the dedicator are introduced and a Berat is obtained, and the Mutevelli by virtue of that Berat, pay money out of the income of the vaqf towards those grants, those expenses are not allowed, the Mutevelli is liable to make compensation for the money given by him.

For unusual expenditure.

ART. 333.—The expenditure of the Mutevelli which is above the customary sum is not allowed.

SECTION II.

Compromise and release of debt by a Mutevelli.

Compromise of action, when allowed.

ART. 334.—If after diligent enquiry it is shewn, that in an action about a thing belonging to the vaqf it is impossible for the Mutevelli to bring proofs and the defendant is willing to take an oath, a compromise for the benefit of the vaqf is allowed.

E.g. If a Mutevelli of a vaqf bring an action about a property held by someone asserting that it belongs to the vaqf, and, when the defendant denies is not able to bring proofs, but it is certain that the defendant will take an oath, the compromise made by the Mutevelli with the defendant, whether for a small or large sum is valid. After the agreement of compromise, the Mutevelli can no longer impose an oath on the defendant.

Nevertheless, if a Mutevelli after the compromise find proofs supporting his action and produce them, then the compromise is set aside.

ART. 335.—If it is certain that one, who is bringing an action about property against the vaqf has proofs, and that judgment will be given against the vaqf, a compromise made by the Mutevelli by payment of a sum out of the property of the vaqf is valid.

Compromise by payment.

ART. 336.—If the Mutevelli of a vaqf agree with its debtor for a part of the debt by a release of the balance, the following conditions are observed :

Release of part of a debt.

If the debt has its origin in an agreement made by the Mutevelli himself, the agreement and release of debt are valid. But for the balance of the sum due under the agreement the Mutevelli must indemnify the dedication.

If the debt did not arise from an agreement made by the Mutevelli himself, then the agreement and release of debt are invalid.

Consequently, in the case of such an agreement and release of debt as aforesaid, the Mutevelli recovers from the debtor the whole of the debt fully.

A compromise is looked upon as invalid, if the debtor confesses his debt, or if, although the debtor denies it, the Mutevelli has proofs.

In default however of confession and proofs, the validity of the compromise is determined as above stated.

Section III.

Liability of a Mutevelli for things in his possession and about matters confirmed by the oath of the Mutevelli.

ART. 337.—The Mutevelli holds as a bailee and not as an insurer. Consequently, if property of the dedication in his possession is damaged or destroyed, without fault or neglect on his part, he is not liable to make compensation (Mejellé 768, 777, 813).

Mutevelli a bailee.

ART. 338.—When, on the death of a Mutevelli of dedicated money, the money, which as principal he received in his lifetime in his character of Mutevelli, is found existing in the estate he leaves, it is handed to his successor. In the case in which this money is not found in the estate he leaves, the following rules are observed :

Recovery from estate (terike) of Mutevelli after death.

If the dead Mutevelli, while he was alive, said that with that money he had bought such an estate for the vaqf or that he had lent such monies to such a person, or that they were lost in his hands without any fault of his, and so it is shewn in some way that he declared something about the fate of that money, indemnification is not due from his estate.

But if he did not declare anything about the fate of that money but died concealing it, then indemnification must be made from his estate.

But if the money which the Mutevelli received when he was alive was not the principal money of the dedication, but interest and income, and he died concealing them, his estate is not bound to make indemnification.

Proof of accounts.

ART. 339.—The Mutevelli of a vaqf authenticates by his oath the fact that he spent out of the income of the dedication a customary sum. He has no need of proof.

Proof of claim.

But when it is a question of paying back money out of dedicated property, his oath is not received, and proofs are required.

E.g. When a Mutevelli of a vaqf is discharged and another is appointed in his place, if the former Mutevelli assert that during his Mutevelliship he spent out of his own property, for the affairs of the vaqf, a fixed customary sum of money, on the condition that the same should be returned to him, and with the advice of the judge, and bring an action against the Mutevelli then acting, his word does not authenticate his statement. Proof is required from him.

SECTION IV.

When the money of one vaqf may be expended on another.

Expenditure on other foundation not allowed.

ART. 340.—It is not lawful, nor is it allowed, that the income of one vaqf, which is limited to a certain object, should be spent for the expenses of another vaqf limited to another object, even if the dedicator should be one and the same person. If the Mutevelli so spend it, he is liable to make good the amount.

E.g. If a man build two schools and dedicate them, and assign to each of them its own properties, it is not permitted to expend money out of the income of the properties of one of the schools on the expenses of the other school.

When surplus monies may be spent.

ART. 341.—It is allowed by the Sacred Law to spend money out of the surplus of the profits of one vaqf for the necessities of another if both the founder of the two vaqfs is one person and the objects of the vaqfs are the same, and the income of one of the vaqfs has diminished.

E.g. If a man dedicates a property and directs that its income is to be spent on the repairs of a school which he has built and dedicated, and dedicates another property appointing that its income should be spent on the pay of the schoolmasters of that school, after a time when the income of the property appointed for the payment of the schoolmasters diminishes, and is not sufficient for their pay, it is allowed to expend on their pay a sum out of the property limited to the repairs of the school.

Income of ruined foundation spent on another by leave of the judge.

ART. 342.—It is allowed, with the permission of the judge, that the income of a ruined and useless vaqf should be spent on another vaqf, whether the dedicators are the same or different (*see* next Chapter).

Section V.
Charitable institutions which have become useless.

ART. 343.—When a vaqf which is a charitable establishment is ruined and rendered useless, it is allowed by the law that its income may, with the leave of the judge, be expended on the expenses of another vaqf of the same sort, nearer in locality and having small income.

E.g. If a school built in a place and dedicated by irrevocable dedication is wholly destroyed by the lapse of time, and the inhabitants of that place are scattered and so the school is rendered useless, its income can be spent, with the leave of the judge, on the necessary expenses of another dedicated school near to it, having small income.

It is not allowed however to spend the income of a vaqf which has become useless on another vaqf of a different sort.

E.g. It is not permitted to spend the income of a hospital which has become useless on schools, or the income of a school which has been destroyed and rendered useless on a hospital.

ART. 344.—If the inhabitants of a village are entirely dispersed and thus the Mesjid in that village is rendered useless, the inhabitants of another village, in which there is no Mesjid and which is near the first, can pull down the Mesjid in the first village, take its material and re-erect it in their own village, and furnish a Mesjid there.

In such a case, the income of the Mesjid pulled down is spent, with the leave of the judge, on the necessities of the Mesjid in the second village.

In the above case, the heirs of the dedicator cannot contend that, since the Mejid was pulled down, its income belongs to them, and that consequently they can take its income and not expend it for the benefit of the Mesjid erected in the other village.

Again, if a Mejsid is dedicated by someone and another person dedicates a sum of money for its wants, and after a lapse of time all the inhabitants of the village are entirely dispersed and the Mesjid falls down, but the Mutevelli wishes to expend the interest of this money, with the leave of the judge, on another Mesjid, in a near village, and having small income, the heirs of the person who dedicated the money, cannot, by reason that the Mesjid, for the benefit of which the money was dedicated, has been destroyed and rendered useless, and that consequently the money is come to them as inheritance, interfere with the Mutevelli.

Section VI.
Borrowing powers of Mutevelli.

ART. 345.—Borrowing is effected either by the receipt of a loan or the purchase of a thing on credit.

Margin notes:
- Income of ruined foundation spent on another, of same sort, near and poor.
- Removal of Mesjid.
- Borrowing, what is.

ART. 346.—If the property of a vaqf has need of repair and the vaqf has no income, the following rules are observed :—

If the dedicator put a term in the deed of dedication that, in necessity the Mutevelli might borrow for the vaqf, then the Mutevelli of his own motion may borrow to spend on the repairs.

If the dedicator has not inserted such a term. the taking of a loan for the vaqf is dependent on the leave of the judge, consequently in such a case, the Mutevelli cannot of his own motion without the leave of the judge, borrow for the vaqf.

ART. 347.—If, when repairs are necessary for the property of a vaqf which has no income to expend, it is not possible to borrow without paying interest, the Mutevelli, by order of the judge, borrows the money at interest in a lawful way, and spends the reasonable sum on the repairs.

In such a case the Mutevelli receives both the principal and interest out of the income of the dedication.

ART. 348.—If a Mutevelli, with the leave of the judge, for the repair of a vaqf property, spend a reasonable sum out of his own money, upon the condition that he is to take again from the vaqf, he takes his expenses from the income of the vaqf.

If he die before he receives it, his heirs take the money expended, on production of proof, from the income of the vaqf and from the Mutevelli appointed in the place of the dead man.

ART. 349.—It is not allowed to take a loan to be used in grants to the officials and beneficiaries.

Consequently, if the Mutevelli borrow money and spend it on grants for the beneficiaries, he ought to repay the creditor the sum which he borrowed out of his own money, he cannot take it from the income of the vaqf.

But if the Mutevelli spend out of his own money sums for grants to the beneficiaries, upon the condition that he was to receive it from the vaqf by the order of the judge, then he can receive his money so expended from the vaqf.

SECTION VII.

Dedicated money.

ART. 350.—If money is dedicated on the condition that it is to be lent to those in need, without interest being charged, the Mutevelli cannot lend it out at interest.

ART. 351.—If the Mutevelli lend money, dedicated with the condition that it shall be let out at interest, and does not stipulate for interest, he cannot take anything as interest from the person to whom it is lent. If in such a case the debtor gives a sum to the Mutevelli as interest, he may calculate it as payment of the principal.

But nevertheless, if the debtor give a sum of money to the Mutevelli and tell him that it is the produce of the money and that he can spend it for the needs of the dedication, and the Mutevelli expend it for that purpose, then the debtor cannot calculate that money towards payment of the principal.

ART. 352.—Interest runs as long as the debt is unpaid. *Interest runs while the debt is unpaid.*
Therefore as long as the debtor owes the debt, interest also is due.

E.g. If the Mutevelli of dedicated money lend a certain sum of money and agree for interest for five years and after one year the debtor dies, and two years pass without the principal sum being paid to the Mutevelli out of the estate of the debtor, when the Mutevelli takes the said sum from the estate, he is entitled to take in addition to the principal the interest earned for the time past up to the time of payment.

In such a case, the heirs of the deceased cannot contend, that by the death of the debtor the interest ceased, and that consequently they are not bound to pay interest for the time which has elapsed after the death of the person from whom they inherit.

ART. 353.—If the Mutevelli of money dedicated to be *Succeeding Mutevelli can sue.* let out at interest, lend some of it, and, before he receives the money from the debtor, is discharged or dies, when another person is appointed in his place, the Mutevelli, for the time being, can take the said money from the debtors.

ART. 354.—The debt due to a vaqf from a deceased *Dedication has no preference over other creditors.* person, who leaves debts in excess of his estate, cannot be preferred to the rest of the debts.

The Mutevelli of the vaqf ranks as other creditors towards the body of creditors.

ART. 355.—Debts are paid by money similar to that *Payment of debts.* which is lent.

Consequently if a man is lent a fixed sum of Turkish pounds out of dedicated money, and expends and consumes them on his necessities, when the Mutevelli of the vaqf claims for the debtor similar pounds, the latter cannot say that he does not give pounds and offer silver mejidies or metaliqs of equal worth with the pounds.

And on the other hand, if the debtor is lent silver mejidies or metaliqs, the trustee cannot claim Turkish pounds of equal value with the sum lent.

Nevertheless, in such a case, after the debtor has voluntarily paid his debt to the Mutevelli in Turkish pounds, he cannot change his mind and demand the return of the Turkish pounds and pay the debt in coins like those lent to him.

CHAPTER XI.
Grants (Vazaif, see Art. 21).

Grants, two sorts.
ART. 356.—Grants made as directed by the dedicator out of the income of the dedicated property are divided into two categories :—

(*a*) grants made for work done.

(*b*) grants made not for work done.

Grant for work done.
ART. 357.—A grant made for work done is looked upon as a wage.

Consequently, if the person entitled to a grant out of the dedication for work done, forsake that work without lawful reason for a time, he is not entitled to take the grant for that time.

Again, if after the person, entitled to a grant for work of some office connected with the dedication, has performed for some years the duties of that office, and taken from the income of the dedication the grant to which he was entitled, another person appears, who asserts that that office was appointed for his benefit, and brings an action and proves his contention, and consequently the office is given to him, the latter cannot recover back the grant for the years during which he did not discharge the duties, which the preceding occupier of the office took, on the ground only that the office belongs to him.

Grant not for work.
ART. 358.—For the grant given not against work, the circumstances of the person, in whose favour it was limited, are considered.

Gift or alms.
If he is rich, the grant is looked upon as a gift.

If he is poor, the grant is looked upon as alms.

Arrears not payable out of subsequent year.
ART. 359.—The grants of each year are paid out of the income of that year.

The grants of one year cannot be paid out of the income of another year.

That is to say, if no income is derived from the dedicated property for one year and for this reason the grants of that year are not paid, but the second year abundant income is derived, the beneficiaries, after taking the grant for the second year, cannot demand out of the surplus the grant also for the first year.

If in such a case the Mutevelli, thinking that payment of the grant for the first year ought to be made out of the income of the second year, pay a sum to the beneficiaries out of the income of the second year on account of the grants of the first year, he takes it back from the beneficiaries.

But if the dedicator insert a stipulation that the grants of one year are to be paid out of the income of another year, it is allowed to pay the grants out of the income of another year.

Art. 360.—The Mutevelli pays away the income of the dedication in the same way as he receives it.

E.g. If the Mutevelli collect the rents of dedicated houses, at the current rate in the city of the Turkish pounds at 108 piastres, he will pay to the beneficiaries at the same rate, the beneficiaries cannot demand payment of their grants at the rate of 100 piastres the pound.

And, on the other hand, in this case, the Mutevelli cannot give the beneficiaries the Turkish pound at 110 or 120 piastres.

Payments made at the same rate as the money was received.

Art. 361.—If the dedicator of money impose as a condition that in case the dedicated money diminishes, the grants are not to be given to the beneficiaries until the principal is raised by the accumulation of interest, if the principal becomes diminished, the Mutevelli cannot give the grant to the beneficiaries, until the full principal is raised by the interest. If he do so, he is liable to make good the amount (*see* Art. 331).

Condition to maintain principal sum.

Art. 362.—If the Mutevelli of a vaqf do not lend the money at interest, and expend on grants to the beneficiaries a sum out of the principal, he is liable to make good the amounts.

In such a case, the Mutevelli, after payment of the indemnification, cannot make a demand upon the beneficiaries for the monies which he paid.

Mutevelli to make good payment out of principal.

Art. 363.—If the income of the vaqf does not cover the expenses, the economies possible are practised by the leave of the judge.

That is to say, if the income of the dedication is much reduced and is not sufficient for its expenses, the Mutevelli applies to the judge.

The judge abolishes altogether out of the grants of the dedication those which are not important, and diminishes those which are important as far as they admit of it.

In such a case, the Mutevelli acts according to the decision of the judge until the pecuniary condition of the dedication is bettered, and after that he pays the grants strictly according to the conditions made by the dedicator.

Where income does not cover expenses.

Art. 364.—If the grant, limited originally by the dedicator, for the servants of the dedication, is not sufficient,

Additions to wages when necessary.

according to the circumstances of the time, for their support, and they are of good conduct and apply themselves to their work, and it is clear that if their pay is not increased they will resign, and that if these resign other competent persons will not be found to do their work for the same pay, and that so the work of the vaqf will remain undone, with the leave of the judge a sufficient sum is added to the grant of the servant out of the surplus (Art. 165).

Dismissed person entitled to grant until notice.

ART. 365.—A person dismissed from his place but performing the duties of the place until his dismissal is made known to him, is entitled to take the grant for that place until the time when his dismissal is made known to him.

From surplus, a sum is set aside for repairs.

ART. 366.—From the surplus which is directed to be given to any persons, certain sums are kept as a reserve for the repair of the dedicated property.

E.g. Even if the property of the vaqf has no need of repair at present, and the surplus of dedication, beyond the fixed expenses, is limited in favour of the children of the dedicator, the Mutevelli keeps out of the surplus a suitable sum as a reserve, that, in case of necessity, he may expend it on the repair of the dedicated property, and gives the rest according to the conditions made by the dedicator to his children.

Mutevelli cannot recover back money paid to beneficiaries.

ART. 367.—After the Mutevelli of a vaqf, of which the surplus is limited in favour of the children of the dedicator, has paid to the children a sum of money as surplus of the dedication, he cannot afterwards, on the allegation that he paid that sum out of his own money, with the intention of taking it out of the surplus, and that no surplus income was derived, take back those monies from the children.

Year, how calculated.

ART. 368.—The beginning of the year, as regards dedications whose produce is annual, is calculated from the ripening of the fruits, and the first day of the second year from the end of the first year.

Grants accrue daily.

ART. 369.—If the possessor of a grant out of a dedication whose produce is annual, die in the middle of a year, the time elapsed from the beginning of the year till the date of his death is calculated and there is given to his heirs a proportional grant.

Right of children born subsequently.

ART. 370.—Where the income of a vaqf producing annual profits is limited in favour of the children of the dedicator, those children of the dedicator, who are born after half the year is passed, are not entitled to share in the income of the year.

But the children of a dedicator born before the lapse of the half year are entitled to take a proportional part of the profits from the day of their birth.

The same rule applies to grandchildren.

ART. 371.—If the dedicator limit the income of his dedicated property in favour of his poor descendants or relations, it is paid to those who happen to be poor when the income arises, whether they were poor before it was made or not. *[margin: Poor, means poor when income is made.]*

Consequently, if one of the descendants or relations of the dedicator happens to be poor as aforesaid before the income arises, and is in good circumstances at the time when the income is made, he takes no share out of the income of the dedication.

On the other hand, a share of the income is given to one who is rich before the income arises, if he has become poor at the time when it is made.

If, however, for some reason the income is not divided for some years, and is going to be divided afterwards, it is expended for those remaining poor at the time of division. Whether they were poor at the time when the income of those years was made or not.

CHAPTER XII.
Appointments (Jihet).
SECTION I.
The giving of appointments.

ART. 372.—Every place of service in a charitable institution, such as the post of Imam, Khatib, Teacher, Preacher, Qayim, is called " Jihet," plural " Jihat." *[margin: Jihet.]*

ART. 373.—It is not allowed to appoint an unfit person to a post. *[margin: Appointee must be a fit person.]*

Consequently, if a person is unfit to discharge the duties of a post, he is dismissed from the post and it is granted to a fit person.

ART. 374.—It is not allowed that a post, limited for the benefit of men who belong to one class, should be granted to men of another class. *[margin: Must be granted to person of the class directed.]*

E.g. A place, appointed to be granted to the Ulemas of the Hanefi doctrine, cannot be given to one of the Shafi'i, nor can a place appointed for the Shafi'i be given to a Hanefi.

Again, a place limited to a Sheykh of the class Naqshbendi, cannot be given to a Sheykh of the class Shazeliye, and on the other hand, a place limited to one of the class Shazeliye cannot be given to one of the class Naqshbendi.

If such an appointment is made by any chance, it is revoked and the place is granted according to the condition of the dedicator.

Death of appointee.

ART. 375.—If the occupier of a place die, leaving a child of full age and able to discharge the duties of the post, this child is appointed to it and not another.

But if the child of the dead man is not competent to discharge the duties of that post, and his unfitness is proved before the judge in his presence, then this post is not given to him, but to another, who is competent.

In such a case, the incompetent child of the dead man cannot interfere with this post by reason that it is his paternal bread.

Transfer of appointment.

See Art. 306, 307.

ART. 376.—The transfer of posts is allowed, but their grant must be made by the judge.

That is to say, if the ability of the man to whom the transfer is made, is proved, and it is not granted to him by the judge at the time of the transfer, the transfer has no force.

A person cannot hold two posts of which the duties are to be performed at the same time.

ART. 377.—It is not allowed for one person to hold two places the duties of which have to be performed at the same time.

Consequently if two places are granted to one person which according to the above rule cannot be held together, that person keeps at his will one of the places and he is made to resign the other.

Where Mutevelli has power to appoint and dismiss.

ART. 378.—If the dedicator direct that the Mutevelli shall appoint and dismiss the officials of the dedication, the judge cannot interfere in the grant of the offices of that dedication, unless the Mutevelli proceed to do some act contrary to law, such as the appointment of an incompetent person, or the dismissal of a person from his office without lawful cause.

In such a case, the judge interferes.

Second appointment.

ART. 379.—If after the grant of an office to one person, it is granted to another, without there being any reason for the dismissal of the first, the office belongs to the person first appointed and not to the second.

But if when there is cause to dismiss the first person appointed, he is dismissed from the office and another person is appointed, then the second appointment is good.

SECTION II.

Deputation of the office and discontinuance from acting.

Power of office holder to appoint a proxy.

ART. 380.—In respect to a vaqf office, it is allowed to depute the office and appoint a proxy.

But it must be done with the approval of the judge.

Consequently one is able, even without justifying cause, to appoint, with the sanction of the judge, a proxy competent to carry out the duties of the office which he holds.

The person, who appoints a proxy, has a right to the pay, as long as the proxy performs the duties. If there has been an agreement that the proxy shall be paid for his work, he is paid by the person who appoints him.

But if it is directed by the dedicator, or by the judge at the time of the appointment to an office, that its possessor should discharge its duties personally, then he cannot appoint a proxy unless there is a justifying cause.

If he does so, he has no right to the pay during the time the duties are performed by the proxy.

ART. 381.—Those who, without reason, forsake or neglect vaqf offices to which they are appointed, are dismissed. *Neglect of office (see Art. 321).*

ART. 382.—If the occupier of an appointment go away to another country and thus interrupt his service for more than three months, the following rules are observed. *Absence of appointee.*

If his journey to the other place is with the object of performing a duty incumbent on him, such as a Hajj and the return to his country, he does not lose his post, but the pay during the time of his business is deducted.

But if his going away is not for a necessary journey then he is dismissed.

CHAPTER XIII.
Renting of Vaqfs.

ART. 383.—The letting of a vaqf at a rent to a beneficiary under the dedication is valid. *Property may be let to beneficiary under the trust.*

E.g. If the Mutevelli let a house or workshop, the income derived from which is settled in favour of the children of the dedicator, to one of the dedicator's children, the letting is valid.

ART. 384.—It is not allowed for the Mutevelli of a vaqf to let it, of his own motion, to himself, even for the equivalent rent. *Mutevelli cannot let to himself without the leave of the judge.*

But if the Mutevelli obtain leave from the judge, and the judge let him that property for the equivalent rent, then the letting is valid.

ART. 385.—If the Mutevelli let a property of which he is Mutevelli to relations of his of so near a degree that their evidence would not be admissible in his behalf, even if the letting is for the equivalent rent, the letting is not valid. *Mutevelli cannot let to a relation.*

Consequently, if the Mutevelli let the property of such vaqf to one of his or her relations, ascending or descending, or to her husband or his wife, the letting is not valid.

ART. 386.—The contract of letting is not dissolved by the death of the Mutevelli who agreed to it. *Lease not dissolved by death of Mutevelli.*

E.g. If the Mutevelli let, at a rack rent, for one year, property of the vaqf for which he is Mutevelli and give possession, and die in the middle of the year, the contract of letting is not dissolved.

ART. 387.—If the Mutevelli of a vaqf let and give possession of properties of the vaqf for which he is Mutevelli, but is dismissed or dies before he receives the rents due from the lessees, and another is appointed in his place, the right of recovery of the rents belongs to the Mutevelli then acting.

It does not belong to the Mutevelli who has ceased to act, nor to the heirs of the deceased Mutevelli.

ART. 388.—If the Mutevelli let the property of the vaqf until the expiration of a fixed term and take the whole rent from the lessee, and afterwards is dismissed or dies before the expiration of the term, and another Mutevelli is appointed to his post, the Mutevelli for the time being, when it is proved that the preceding Mutevelli received the whole rent as aforesaid, is not able to demand again rent from the lessor for the time falling within the period of his Mutevelliship.

Because by the receipt of the former Mutevelli, the lessee is released from the obligation to pay.

ART. 389.—The dedicated property must be let at the equivalent rent.

If the Mutevelli let it at a rent less than the value, the following rules are observed :—

If the deficiency is excessive, the lease is invalid.

If the deficiency is small, the lease is valid.

ART. 390.—In the letting, the deficiency of the rent is considered excessive if it is one fifth or more less than the value, it is small if it is less than one fifth below the value.

ART. 391.—When there is necessity to hire something on account of the vaqf it must be hired at the equivalent rent.

Consequently, if the Mutevelli hires something on account of the vaqf, for a rent excessively above the value, the hiring is not valid.

But the validity of the hiring is not prejudiced by a small excess.

In hiring, a rent which is one-fifth or more above the value is considered excessive.

The excess is considered small which is less than one-fifth above the value.

ART. 392.—If the Mutevelli let the dedicated property for a rent excessively below the value, it is required that the value be made good.

If the lessee refuse to make it good, then the Mutevelli dissolves the lease and lets the property to another for the rent according to its value. If the lessee has possessed the property for some time before the lease has been put an end to, the rent according to its value is taken from him for that time.

ART. 393.—If the Mutevelli of a vaqf let it for a fixed time for the equivalent rent, and, afterwards, third persons, for some object offer a sum above that rent and seek to hire it, their offer is not taken into consideration.

After lease granted higher offer not to be accepted. If rent increases 50 per cent. rent to be raised.

But if in the course of the term, by common demand, the value of that property to let has increased to an excessive extent, the hirer is bound to pay the additional rent for the remainder of the term.

With reference to the above matter, an increase of the sum up to the half of the agreed rent is considered an excessive increase.

If in the manner prescribed, the lessee does not consent to pay the additional rent, the Mutevelli dissolves the contract of letting, takes the property out of the hands of the lessee and lets it to the person offering to take it at that rent.

In such a case, if the Mutevelli does not dissolve the contract, and the lessee keeps possession of the property until the expiration of his term, the lessee must pay the rent named for the whole time of the letting.

The Mutevelli cannot ask more from him.

ART. 394.—Neither the Mutevelli nor the beneficiary can let to a third party a property the right to inhabit which is dedicated.

Property in trust for habitation cannot be let.

The cases are excepted in which there is absolute necessity for the vaqf (*see* Art. 165).

Unless necessity.

ART. 395.—When there is a question of a property being let by the Mutevelli to a third person for an equivalent rent, and the income from that property is dedicated, the persons, in whose favour the income is settled, cannot stop the Mutevelli from letting that property, relying on the argument that its income is settled on them and that consequently they can possess and prevent the letting of it to a third person.

Where income dedicated, beneficiary has no right to occupy.

ART. 396.—If the lessee of a dedicated property, which has need of repair in any part, and of which the Mutevelli is abroad, repair by the order of the judge the part having need of repair, expending out of his own money a reasonable sum, on the condition of taking it back from the vaqf, he can set off those expenses against the rent.

Repairs by lessee when recoverable.

ART. 397.—In every case, whether the letting of dedicated property is defective by reason that the rent is unknown, or it is defective because the other conditions

Where lease defective assessed rent to be paid.

I

constituting a valid letting do not exist, the lessee must pay a sum equal to the equivalent rent.

There is no indispensable condition (as there is in the case of properties of pure ownership) in the second case, that the rent must not exceed the rent agreed upon (Mejellé, 462).

Where lease invalid, rack rent to be paid.

ART. 398.—The equivalent rent is due, if the lessee possess the dedicated property, even if the property is let under a letting which is invalid (Mejellé, 459).

Mutevelli can let for rack rent although dedicator direct a different rent.

ART. 399.—If a person dedicating a property direct that it shall not be let for a sum exceeding a fixed sum, the Mutevelli can let it for the equivalent rent even if this is greater than the fixed sum (*see* Art. 389).

If dedicator direct that the poor are to inhabit without paying, the Mutevelli cannot demand rent.

ART. 400.—If a person, who dedicates houses, direct that the poor shall live in them without paying rent, the Mutevelli cannot, contrary to the direction of the dedicator, demand rent from the poor living in those houses by the direction of the judge.

In such a case, if the Mutevelli demand rent from the poor living in those houses, and they pay it to the Mutevelli for any time, thinking that they are bound to do this, they can demand and take it back from the Mutevelli.

Mutevelli cannot revoke lease.

ART. 401.—After the Mutevelli has let dedicated property, he cannot dissolve and upset the letting, if the dissolution of the contract is not more beneficial to the dedication.

If he do so, the dissolution of the contract is not valid.

CHAPTER XIV.
Wrongful appropriation of dedicated property.

Trespasser to make good loss to true vaqf.

ART. 402.—The benefits derived from dedicated property must be refunded.

Consequently, if one by force seize and for a time take possession of a dedicated property, whether it is dedicated to be let at rent or not, in every case he must pay to the vaqf the equivalent rent for the time he possesses it.

E.g. If one wrongfully appropriates or take possession for a time of a dedicated school or college not dedicated to be let at rent, he must pay the equivalent rent of that school or college for that time.

True vaqf land.

But if a man wrongfully appropriates and seizes for a time land which is true vaqf and cultivates it and diminishes the productiveness of the field, then the following rules are observed :—

If the diminution in the productiveness of the field is greater than the equivalent rent, the wrongful appropriator is condemned to pay the diminution in productiveness,

If the equivalent rent is greater than the diminution in productiveness, then he is condemned to pay the equivalent rent.

But since vaqf lands of the Takhsisat category are looked upon as State Lands, and as the wrongful appropriator of State Lands, is not compelled to pay an equivalent rent, and loss of productiveness. *Takhsisat vaqf land.*

So also in respect of vaqf lands of this category he is not compelled to pay them (Land Law, Art. 21).

ART. 403.—It is not allowed to give income bearing vaqf properties as a loan for use. *Borrower of vaqf properties is a trespasser.*

Consequently, if the Mutevelli give to another as a loan for use any thing out of the Mustaghelat of a vaqf, and the person to whom it is lent uses it for a time, the latter is looked upon as a wrongful appropriator and is bound to pay to the vaqf equivalent rent for that time.

ART. 404.—If the person, in whose favour a right to dwell in a dedicated house is exclusively given, let that house to another, the rent belongs to him and not to the vaqf. *Person entitled to occupy may let.*

Consequently, the Mutevelli cannot demand the rent as belonging to the vaqf.

ART. 405.—If one possess a dedicated thing wrongfully, although he claims such possession under an agreement or as owner, he must pay the equivalent rent. *Person ejected must pay rent for time of occupation.*

E.g. If one buy from another for a known price a property and take and possess it for a time, and afterwards the Mutevelli of some vaqf bring an action and prove that the property belongs to the vaqf of which he is Mutevelli, and, according to the Sacred Law, judgment is given in favour of the vaqf, the purchaser must pay the equivalent rent for the time he possessed the property.

In such a case, the purchaser cannot refuse payment of the equivalent rent, for the reason that he possessed that property under a claim of ownership, because he had bought it.

Also, if a person take exclusive possession of a property by force, for a time, and half of it belongs to him and the other half to the vaqf, he must pay an equivalent rent for the half share belonging to the vaqf during the time he possessed it.

ART. 406.—The wrongful appropriator must pay the equivalent rent, even if he did not enjoy the benefits of the thing appropriated. *Rent to be paid though no profit derived.*

E.g. If a man wrongfully appropriates, for a time, dedicated land, but gets no profit from it, leaving it unemployed, he must pay the equivalent rent for that land to the vaqf for the time he held it as a wrongful appropriator.

I2

Again if one get no benefit from a dedicated house or workshop which he has appropriated, leaving them closed, he must pay to the vaqf the equivalent rent of the house or workshop for as long as the appropriation lasted.

Destruction of vaqf property.

ART. 407.—If one without right and by force destroy a property constituting a charitable establishment, such as a school or place of worship, he must rebuild it as before.

But if he forcibly pull down a building of vaqf Mustaghelat, he is condemned to make compensation according to its value when standing. He is not compelled to build the house as before.

Trespass by joint beneficiary.

ART. 408.—If one of those to whom the right of occupying dedicated property is given, by force and to the exclusion of others dwell in it for a time without the leave of the others, the latter take from the person, exclusively occupying the house equivalent rent according to their shares.

CHAPTER XV.

Repairs and buildings in relation to dedicated property.

SECTION I.

Repairs of dedicated property made by the beneficiary when the right to inhabit the property is settled on him.

Additions by persons entitled to occupy not given to dedication.

ART. 409.—If the person, in whose favour the occupation of a dedicated house is limited, execute at his own expense such works as can be separated from the house (*see* Art. 30) without giving them to the dedication, these are looked upon as his property.

Consequently, if in the case of a dedicated house the occupation of which is limited in favour of the Ulema, the person, who by judicial grant dwells in it, builds and at his own expense adds certain buildings for himself, and after this dies, the building belongs to his heirs.

In such a case, if this house is granted to another of the Ulema, he becomes owner of that building and pays its value to the heirs of the deceased.

In the case in which he refuses to pay the value of that building, the judge lets the house to another until its value is derived from the rent.

As soon as its value is fully and completely made from the rent, the house belongs to the person to whom the house was granted.

Additions given to the vaqf.

ART. 410.—If the person, in whose favour the occupation of a dedicated house is limited while he is in a state of good health, erect buildings at his own expense in addition to that house, and it is attested by witnesses that he builds it as a gift for the vaqf and he afterwards dies, his heirs cannot claim those buildings on the alleged reason that they passed to them by inheritance.

If the person in whose favour the occupation of a house is limited effect in respect of it certain work of the sort which cannot be separated (*see* Art. 29), at his own expense, in every case he is considered to have given it to the vaqf. *Person entitled to occupy.*

ART. 411.—The expenses of repairs take precedence of grants (*see* Chapter XI). *Repairs take precedence of grants.*

Consequently, when there is need to repair a dedicated property, the income which there is cannot be spent on grants.

In such a case, if the Mutevelli spent what income there is on grants and nothing remains for repairs, he is liable to make good the sum which he expended on grants.

ART. 412.—If a house, the right of occupying which is dedicated, is ruined, the following rules are observed:— *House dedicated to be occupied, ruined.*

If the dedicator has imposed a term, that the house is to be repaired out of the income of the vaqf, then it is repaired, in accordance with that term, out of such income of the vaqf as there is.

But if the dedicator has not imposed any such term, or if he has imposed such a term, but there is no income, then the beneficiary repairs the house at his own expense.

But if the beneficiary cannot pay the cost of the repair, or refuses to pay it, although he is able, the house, with the approval of the judge, is let by the Mutevelli to another, in order that it may be repaired out of the rents received.

ART. 413.—If a vaqf building, of which the income is settled on the children of the dedicator, fall into ruin and have need of repair, the Mutevelli will spend the income derived on the repairs. The children cannot refuse their assent to this and demand the division of the income among themselves. *Repair of building of which the income is dedicated.*

SECTION II.

Buildings erected on dedicated land.

ART. 414.—If the Mutevelli erect a building on the land of the vaqf, the following rules are observed:— *Building by Mutevelli.*

If the money spent on the building belongs to the vaqf, the building in every case belongs to the vaqf, whether the Mutevelli has declared and had it witnessed when the building was erected that he built for himself or for the vaqf or not.

If the money expended does not belong to the vaqf but to the Mutevelli, then, if at the time of the erection, he has declared and it has been witnessed that it is built for himself, the building belongs to the Mutevelli.

But if when the building is being erected, the Mutevelli does not declare and cause it to be witnessed that he is building for himself, and keeps silence, then the building belongs to the vaqf.

But when the Mutevelli who has raised a building at his own expense is himself the dedicator, even if, while it was being built, he did not declare and cause it to be witnessed that he built it for himself and kept silence, that building becomes his property.

Building by person other than the Mutevelli.

ART. 415.—If a person, not being the Mutevelli, erect a building on vaqf land at his own expense, in every case the building is his property, whether he declares and causes it to be witnessed at the time of the building that he was building for himself or keep silence.

CHAPTER XVI.
Exchange of dedicated property.

Exchange when allowed.

ART. 416.—The exchange of a vaqf property is not allowed if the dedicator has not inserted a term authorizing its exchange.

But if that property does not produce any income for the vaqf, or its income does not cover its expenses, and so it is shewn that a change will benefit the vaqf, then, even, if the dedicator has expressly forbidden a change, the change is allowed with the approval of the judge and the leave of the Sultan (*see* Art. 165).

Property taken in exchange must have a situation of equal reputation.

ART. 417.—The mulk property taken as the price must not be inferior to the vaqf property as regards situation and reputation.

Consequently, the situation of the mulk property must, as regards reputation, be equal to or better than that of the vaqf property.

If it is worse, the exchange is not valid.

E.g. An exchange of vaqf property situated in Diwan Yol for mulk property situated in Qasim Pasha or in Yeni Baghcha is invalid even if the latter be greater in extent and produces a greater income than the vaqf property.

Need not be in the same city.

ART. 418.—In order that an exchange may be valid, it is not an indispensable condition, that the mulk property taken in exchange and the vaqf property should be situated in the same city.

Consequently, the exchange of vaqf property situated in one city for mulk property in another is valid.

E.g. A valid exchange can be made of vaqf property situated in Constantinople for mulk property in Smyrna, which has a better reputation and greater value.

ART. 419.—It is allowed to change dedicated property for cash. *Exchange for cash.*

ART. 420.—It is not allowed to retract from an exchange judicially declared valid. *Exchange when irrevocable.*

That is to say, if a vaqf property is exchanged by the leave of the judge and by the order of the Sultan, and the approval of the Mutevelli, the conditions required for an exchange being in existence, and after the judge has decided after a hearing about the validity and irrevocability of the exchange, it is not allowed to retract from this exchange.

CHAPTER XVII.

Actions relating to vaqfs contains two Chapters.

SECTION I.

When an action will lie.

ART. 421.—An action will lie for the price of the grant of vaqf immovable property held in Ijaretein (*see* Art. 223). *An action will lie for the price of Ijareteinle.*

ART. 422.—If a person brings an action claiming to be a descendant or relation of the dedicator, he must set out the ties of relationship between himself and the dedicator. If he is unable to do so, his action is dismissed. *A person claiming as descendant from a dedicator must set out his descent from the dedicator.*

ART. 423.—If a Mutevelliship, limited in favour of the descendants of a dedicator, becomes vacant, and someone appears and claims that he is a descendant of the dedicator, and consequently brings an action about the Mutevelliship, his action is dismissed, unless he can shew the ties of relationship between himself and the dedicator.

That is to say. his action is dismissed if he do not say, " such a one is my father, and such a one his father, and such a dedicator his father," and so trace the genealogical relationship which he holds to the dedicator, shewing and enumerating the names of the persons intervening between himself and the dedicator, and allege that he belongs to the family of the dedicator.

When however an action is brought about the descent from a relationship to a person, who is clearly proved to be a descendant of the dedicator, it is not necessary to prove his ties of relationship to the dedicator. *Or from someone clearly proved to be a descendant of the dedicator.*

E.g. When the Mutevelliship of an ancient vaqf is limited in favour of the descendants of the dedicator, and on their failure, in favour of the masters of some school, and the person in possession of the Mutevelliship dies, he being clearly proved to be a descendant of the dedicator, and the master aforesaid, thinking that the heirs of the dedicator have failed, take the office of Mutevelli of this vaqf, and afterwards another person appears alleging that he is a son of the deceased Mutevelli, and so bring an action and offers to prove that he is a son of the deceased, wishing to take this Mutevelliship, the master of the school cannot refuse to retire from the Mutevelliship until the plaintiff has declared and proved the ties of relationship subsisting between himself and the dedicator.

Again, if one person, proved to be the child of the dedicator, holds a post of Mutevelli, which is limited in favour of children of children, and another person appears asserting that he is a son of his full blood brother (nephew) and consequently a descendant of the dedicator, and bring an action and prove it in the manner prescribed by law and desire on this account to share the post of Mutevelli, the defendant cannot refuse to allow him to share on the ground that it is necessary for the plaintiff to declare and prove the ties of relationships between himself and the dedicator.

Again, if one proved to be, *e.g.* a descendant of the fifth generation, holds the post of Mutevelli of a vaqf of which the Mutevelliship and income are limited in favour of the descendants of the dedicator, and another person appears asserting that he is his cousin, and consequently a descendant of the dedicator of the same generation and in the same degree, and he brings an action and proves that he is cousin of the defendant, he shares the Mutevelliship and the income.

In such a case he is not required to declare and prove the bonds of relationship subsisting between the dedicator and himself.

ART. 424.—In an action about a vaqf it is not necessary to make mention of the name of the dedicator.

It is not necessary that the name of the dedicator should be known.

That is to say, when an action is brought about a place as vaqf property, the action lies, even if the name of the dedicator is no longer remembered.

Grant-collateral document.

ART. 425.—If someone grant finally to another, by the leave of the Mutevelli, a vaqf property held in Ijaretein, and it is agreed between the grantor and the grantee that the grant is fictitious and to be looked upon as istiglal (Art. 20) and afterwards the grantor sues the grantee, who denies that the grant was fictitious and asserts that in the presence of the Mutevelli the grantor had made a final grant of the property, the action is heard, if the plaintiff produce a document bearing the signature or seal of the grantee, shewing that the grant was fictitious.

But if he cannot produce such a writing, the judges are forbidden by Imperial Order to hear such action.

Consequently if a judge hear such an action, when no document exists, and receive the plaintiff's witnesses to prove that the grant was istiglal (Art. 20) and decide that the grant was istiglal (Art. 20) his decision is not to be executed.

ART. 426.—When a person has, by leave of the Mute-velli, finally sold a vaqf property which he held in Ijaretein, and the grant has been put into writing, if he afterwards assert that he conveyed it gratis upon the condition that the grantee should support him until his death, and demand the return of the property on the ground that the condition of maintenance has not been performed, and when the grantee refuses, brings an action, it is forbidden to the judges by Imperial decree to hear such actions.

Parole evidence inadmissible to contradict writing.

Consequently, if the judge hear the action and give judgment that the property is to be returned to the plaintiff, his decision is not to be carried out.

(The Imperial Order cited in this article was issued on the 28th Rejeb, 1296, and is after the date of the occupation of Cyprus).

ART. 427.—If one grant to another, by the leave of the Mutevelli, his immovable property held in Ijaretein, and afterwards admit before the judge that he validly granted that property by the leave of the Mutevelli, and the judge give to the grantee a valid title of grant, the action of the grantor will not be heard, if he subsequently repent and sue the grantee on the ground that he conveyed the property upon a defective condition.

Admission of grantor estoppel.

ART. 428.—If one grant to another, by the leave of the Mutevelli, his immovable property held in Ijaretein, and afterwards assert that the grant was fictitious, and when the grantee denies this, the grantor brings an action and produces a written document, admissible in evidence, bearing the signature or seal of the grantee and shewing that the grant is fictitious, the action is heard.

Collateral document.

If after the death of the grantor, his heirs having the right of inheritance in the way above mentioned bring an action and produce a document, their action is heard.

Again, if after the death of the grantee, his heirs having the right of inheritance, take possession of the property, the action of the grantor against the heirs of the grantee is heard, if he produce a document bearing the signature or seal of the grantee.

If both the grantor and grantee die, leaving heirs having the right of inheritance, the action of the heirs of the grantor against the heirs of the grantee is heard, if they bring an action and produce such a document.

But if the grantee die and leave no heirs with the right of inheritance and the property belongs, as being without owner, to the vaqf, an action to prove that the grant was fictitious is not heard, even if the grantor produce such a document.

Estoppel of lessee.

ART. 429.—If one rent and receive from the Mutevelli vaqf property held in Ijaretein, and afterwards bring an action alleging that the property was his own property prior to the letting, his action is not heard.

Estoppel by payment of rent.

ART. 430.—If a person after he has paid rent for a time to a Mutevelli for an immovable property in his possession, on the ground that it belongs to some vaqf, brings an action asserting that the property is his own, his action is not heard.

Estoppel by admission.

ART. 431.—If one grant a vaqf property held in Ijaretein, for a fixed price, by leave of the Mutevelli, to another and confess that he received that price in full, his action brought after this to recover the price is not heard.

Estoppel of vendor.

ART. 432.—If the children of a dead person sell for a known price and deliver to another a property as being their mulk property coming to them from their father's inheritance, and afterwards bring an action, alleging that that property is part of the Mustaghelat of a certain vaqf, that their father during his lifetime possessed it in Ijaretein, that after his death it simply passed to them as inheritance, and that consequently the sale of that property as mulk was not lawful, their action is not heard.

Estoppel by admission.

ART. 433.—When a man appointed Mutevelli confesses that he has received a certain sum of money from the vaqf property, and afterwards after the lapse of some time, when the accounts are examined, asserts that he did not receive such money, and that his previous confession is false, if he bring an action about this it is not heard.

Release a bar.

ART. 434.—After one has granted to another vaqf property held in Ijaretein, by the leave of the Mutevelli, and has by release freed the grantee from all actions relating to that property if he afterwards allege that he granted that property by feragh bil vefa and bring an action for this against the grantee, his action is not heard.

SECTION II.

Prescription.

In actions relating to original dedication.

ART. 435.—The time of prescription in actions relating to the corpus of dedicated property is 36 years (Mejellé, 1661).

Consequently an action relating to the corpus is not heard, if it has been omitted to be brought for 36 years.

E.g. If one possess a property for 36 years as his mulk property, with the knowledge of the Mutevelli of a vaqf, and the Mutevelli has kept silence during that time, without any reason recognized by the law, the action of the Mutevelli is not heard, if he allege that that property is part of the Mustaghelat of the vaqf of which he was Mutevelli during those years.

Again, if the Mutevelli of one vaqf let for 36 years, with the knowledge of the Mutevelli of another vaqf, a property as belonging to the Mustaghelat of his vaqf, and the Mutevelli of the second vaqf was silent, without an excuse recognized by the law during that time, the action of the Mutevelli of the second vaqf is not heard, if he afterwards brings one against the Mutevelli of the first vaqf alleging that that property is part of the Mustaghelat of the vaqf of which he has been Mutevelli for more than 36 years.

Again, if someone possess for 36 years a field as Arazi mirié, with the knowledge of the Mutevelli of a vaqf, who, without excuse recognized by law, kept silence during this time, the claim of the Mutevelli before the land authorities by which the Mutevelli claims that the field is part of the Mustaghelat of the vaqf of which he has been Mutevelli for those years is not heard.

Likewise, if the Mutevelli of dedicated monies, who lives in one and the same city with another person for 35 years, and keeps silence without excuse during that time and brings no action against him, afterwards brings an action alleging that he has to receive a fixed sum of the monies of the vaqf due before those years, and the person sued defends the action, this action is not heard.

ART. 436.—The prescription in respect of property dedicated in favour of children from generation to generation commences from the time when the first generation fails.

Where property dedicated in favour of children from generation to generation.

E.g. If a vaqf immovable property of which the Mutevelliship and the income is dedicated in favour of the children of the dedicator from generation to generation, is sold by a child of the first generation and delivered to another, and the purchaser receive and possess it for 35 years, and afterwards when the first generation is wholly extinct, the children of the second generation are appointed Mutevellis, and after the lapse of a year they bring an action against the purchaser, alleging that the property is vaqf, this action is heard.

Because one year scarcely has passed since the first generation became extinct.

The time passed before this epoch is not counted in the time of prescription.

Again, if, with the knowledge of the children of the first generation, a stranger take for 14 years the Mutevelliship, which the dedicator limited to his children and descendants from generation to generation, and afterwards, when the first generation is extinct, the children of the second generation after the lapse of one year bring an action against the stranger claiming the Mutevelliship, the stranger cannot demand the dismissal of the action on the ground that it is not heard after the lapse of 15 years.

Posession of vaqf properties. ART. 437.—The time of prescription for actions relating to the possession (tassaruf) of vaqf properties extends to 15 years (Mejellé, 1660).

Consequently, actions about possession are dismissed if they are omitted to be brought without reason for 15 years.

E.g. If someone possesses for 15 years an Ijaretein vaqf property with the knowledge of another person, who keeps silence during the said time without legal excuse, when the latter person brings an action, alleging that he possessed that property in Ijaretein before that time, his action is dismissed.

Again, if two persons possess in common for 15 years Ijaretein vaqf property and during this period neither of them has brought an action against the other, if at any time afterwards one of them brings an action alleging that before that time he possessed the property in Ijaretein as sole owner, his action is dismissed.

Likewise when someone has taken and possessed, with the knowledge of the Mutevelli, as Ijaretein a vaqf property for 15 years, and the Mutevelli during this period has kept silence without legal excuse, if afterwards he brings an action, alleging, that that property was not rented to this man and that he seized it without authority, the action of the Mutevelli is dismissed (Mejellé, 1660).

Vaqf money. ART. 438.—The time of prescription for actions relating to the corpus of monies made vaqf extends to 36 years (Mejellé, 1661).

But the time of prescription in actions relating to the interest of such monies extends to 15 years (Mejellé, 1660).

Possession by different persons, grantor and grantee. ART. 439.—The time of possession of the grantor and that of the grantee are added together and calculated together.

That is to say, if the grantor possess Mustaghelat vaqf property for a time, and the grantee possesses it for a time, and the sum of the two times completes the period of prescription, the action of a plaintiff who has omitted to bring it during those times without legal excuse is dismissed.

E.g. When someone has seized vaqf Mustaghelat and held it as Ijaretein tenant for 15 years with the knowledge of a second person, and afterwards has conveyed it to another, who again has possessed it for five years with the knowledge of the person aforesaid, and that person has kept silence during both these periods without legal excuse, if afterwards that person brings an action asserting that he possessed that property before those times as Ijaretein tenant, his action is dismissed because there is prescription.

ART. 440.—The times of possession of the heir and the person from whom he inherits are added together and calculated together (Mejellé, 1670). Ancestor and heir.

That is to say, if someone die after he has possessed vaqf property by Ijaretein for a certain time, and his heirs having the right of inheritance, take and possess that property in Ijaretein relying simply on their rights of succession, and the aggregate of these two periods completes the time of prescription, the action of the plaintiff is dismissed, if he has kept silence during those times without legal excuse.

ART. 441.—The fact that the defendant proceeds to other defences does not interfere with the objection of prescription to the action of the plaintiff. Prescriptions may be relied on although other defences raised.

E.g. When someone has possessed property on an Ijaretein tenure without dispute for 15 years to the knowledge of another person, and afterwards that person brings an action, asserting that he possessed that property before those years and that the possessor has taken it by wrongful appropriation, the objection of the defendant on account of prescription is not rejected if he say that in fact that property was possessed formerly by the plaintiff, on an Ijaretein tenure, but that 15 years before with the leave of the Mutevelli, he made a final conveyance of the property to him.

Consequently, proof of the defence of the defendant is not required but the property is preserved in his possession.

ART. 442.—When someone, after he has possessed property for 36 years and more, is sued by the Mutevelli of a vaqf who asserts that that property is part of the Mustaghelat of the vaqf of which he is Mutevelli and that he let it to the defendant during that time. And if the defendant deny the action of the Mutevelli and assert that that property is his own mulk property, the following rules are observed: Where Mutevelli asserts owner is lessee.

If it is known to the world that the vaqf had leased that property during that time, the action of the Mutevelli is heard.

If it is not known, then the action is dismissed.

ART. 443.—The time of prescription, to cause the dismissal of actions, must pass without action brought (Mejellé, 1666). Prescription runs to time of action brought.

Consequently, if one sue another, for a certain matter, before the judge, but the action is not decided and so the time of prescription is completed, this prescription does not prevent the action being heard.

It is required, nevertheless, that the time intervening between the two actions should not complete the time of prescription.

If the intervening time completes the time of prescription, the action is dismissed.

E.g. If one sue another before the judge, alleging that the defendant a year before granted him a certain vaqf property, which he before owned as Ijaretein, by the leave of the Mutevelli, and claim the delivery of the property, and the defendant disputes the claim, but when the action is not adjudicated upon, afterwards after the lapse of 10 years, he bring another action before the judge for the same matter, and again it is not adjudicated upon as also before, and then seven other years pass, an action brought after this for the same matter is heard.

But if, in the first case, he bring an action after the lapse of 15 years from the first action, the action is dismissed, because the time elapsed between the two actions, completes the time of prescription.

Ignorance of title no excuse. ART. 444.—In prescription, ignorance is not looked upon as a valid justification for silence.

E.g. If one hold the Mutevelliship of a vaqf for 15 years, with the knowledge of another, who keeps silence without legal excuse during that time, and the latter person afterwards brings an action alleging that before those years the post of Mutevelli according to the direction of the dedicator belonged to him, but that he was not able to bring his action for this, because he did not know the direction of the dedicator and that now he proceeds to the action, this action is dismissed.

A Mutevelli cannot make an admission against the vaqf. ART. 445.—The admission of the Mutevelli of a vaqf against that vaqf is not valid and no effect is to be given to it.

Consequently, prescription is not prevented by the admission of the Mutevelli against the vaqf.

That is to say, if the Mutevelli of a vaqf take and possess a property, as Mustaghelat of the vaqf for 15 years, with the knowledge of another person, who keeps silence during this time without legal excuse, and, when that person afterwards brings an action, asserting that that property was before those years his mulk property, the Mutevelli admits the contention of the plaintiff, the prescription in respect of that action is not prevented. Consequently the action of the plaintiff is dismissed.

Again, if the Mutevelli of a vaqf take and possess for 36 years a property as part of the Mustaghelat of the vaqf, with the knowledge of the Mutevelli of another vaqf, who keeps silence during that time, without legal excuse, when afterwards the latter brings an action against the Mutevelli of the first vaqf, alleging that that property is part of the Mustaghelat of the vaqf of which he is Mutevelli, if the Mutevelli of the first vaqf admit that the property, the subject of the litigation, belongs to the Mustaghelat of the second vaqf, this does not prevent the action of the Mutevelli of the second vaqf being barred by prescription.

Consequently, the action of the Mutevelli of the second vaqf is dismissed.

ART. 446.—The time of the prescription of actions for interest and income is 15 years. *Prescription in action for interest or income.*

Consequently an action for interest or income, which, without legal excuse, the Mutevelli has omitted to bring for 15 years, is dismissed.

ART. 447.—The time of prescription in action relating to the possession of vaqf lands of the Tahksisat category is 10 years. *Possession of vaqf land of Tahksisat category (tassaruf). Reversion (raqabe).*

But the time in actions relating to the reversion in them is 36 years.

ART. 448.—In prescription the lunar year is in force, and not the solar year. *Lunar year.*

Consequently the time of prescription ought to be calculated according to the lunar year.

ART. 449.—In actions about philanthropic establishments appointed for the common benefit, there is no prescription (Mejellé, 1675). *Common establishments no prescription.*

N.B.—As to prescription in actions to recover immoveable property in Cyprus see Acts IV. of 1886, and V. of 1887.

CHAPTER XVIII.
Parties to actions.

ART. 450.—In every action relating to tasarruf or to the possession of Ijaretein vaqf properties, the presence of the Mutevelli is required. Whether the lessee of the estate is plaintiff or defendant. *When presence of Mutevelli is required.*

But in the case of wrongful appropriation of Ijaretein vaqf property, the lessee can bring an action against the wrongful appropriator, without the presence of the Mutevelli being required.

E.g. If one bring an action against another, alleging that he is entitled to the possession (tasarruf) as tenant by Ijaretein of certain vaqf property, part of the Mustaghelat of a vaqf, which is in the possession of the other person, in order that the action may be valid, the presence of the Mutevelli of the vaqf is required.

Again, if one bring an action about a property, held by another on an Ijaretein tenure as Mussaqafat of some vaqf, alleging that that property is his own mulk property, or, that he is Ijaretein tenant, such action is invalid, if the Mutevelli is not present.

Consequently, if the judge hear this action, contrary to the above prohibition, in the absence of the Mutevelli, and give a decision about it his judgment is not to be carried out.

But if someone bring an action about Ijaretein vaqf property held by another, alleging that the defendant wrongfully appropriated and took it, whilst he, the plaintiff, was Ijaretein tenant, the action coming on in the absence of the Mutevelli, is heard.

Where more than the vaqf concerned. ART. 451.—If the vaqf property, the subject matter of the action, is mixed with other vaqfs, the presence of all the Mutevellis of those vaqfs is required. The presence of some only of them is not sufficient.

Muqata'a vaqf. ART. 452.—The presence of the Mutevelli of the vaqf is not required in actions about the buildings and trees comprised in properties of which the land is Muqata'a vaqf and the buildings and trees upon it pure mulk.

But the presence of the Mutevelli is required in an action relating to the land of the vaqf.

Lessee of Ijaretein vaqf can sue without Mutevelli. ART. 453.—If one lets to another his Ijaretein vaqf property and sue the lessee for arrears of rent the presence of the Mutevelli of the vaqf is not required in action.

Actions for price. ART. 454.—The presence of the Mutevelli is not required in actions to recover the price on alienation.

That is to say, if someone bring an action against another alleging that he has to recover from him a fixed sum of money, as the price of such a property, which he has granted to him by the leave of the Mutevelli and which is a Mustaghelat vaqf possessed in Ijaretein, the presence of the Mutevelli is not required in the action.

Action to settle boundaries between two vaqfs. ART. 455.—When one of the holders of two adjacent Ijaretein properties, which belong to different vaqf, brings an action against the other owner for trespassing beyond the boundaries of the property held by him, the presence of the Mutevellis of both vaqfs is required.

Action for damages against wrongful appropriator. ART. 456.—In an action to recover payment of the equivalent rent due by a wrongful appropriator, who has taken possession by force, of a land held in Ijaretein, the litigant is the Mutevelli of the vaqf and not the Ijaretein tenant.

Unless the Mutevelli has appointed the Ijaretein tenant to represent him in this action.

Action about benefit. ART. 457.—In actions about the benefit of a dedication brought by those in whose favour the dedication was made, one of these can be a litigant.

ART. 458.—If someone claims that he also by the terms *Claim to Mutevelliship.* used by the dedicator has a right to the office of Mutevelli held by certain persons as joint owners, one only of those who possess the Mutevelliship is made defendant, the presence of the rest is not required.

Consequently, the judgment given against one of them is of force against the rest.

But in order that the judgment given should bind the rest of the heirs, it is necessary that the claim of the plaintiff should be proved.

E.g. If while certain of the descendants of the dedicator are in possession of the Mutevelliship of a vaqf limited in favour of the children of the dedicator, someone appears and brings an action, in the presence of one only of the possessors of the office, and alleges that he also is a descendant of the dedicator, and proves his claim by evidence, and judgment is given accordingly, this judgment binds also the rest of those who hold the office.

Again, if while certain descendants of the dedicator of the second generation hold the Mutevelliship of the vaqf, limited in favour of the descendants of the dedicator from generation to generation, someone appears and brings an action in the presence of one only of those who hold the office and asserts that he is a child of the dedicator of the first generation and proves his claim in the manner required by law, the judgment given in his favour binds also the rest of those who hold the office.

Consequently, in such a case, all those who hold the Mutevelliship are dismissed and it is awarded to the plaintiff.

ART. 459.—If two persons claim a Mutevelliship which is *Opposing claim to Mutevelliship.* vacant, while the person in whose favour it is given by the terms used by the dedicator is not yet fixed, the claim cannot be tried in an action between these two persons.

Consequently, a representative of the vaqf is appointed by the judge in whose presence action is brought.

ART. 460.—In action about vaqf properties of which *Mutevelli to sue, not beneficiary.* the rent or right of occupation is dedicated, the Mutevelli of the vaqf must be a party to the action and not the person in whose favour the rent or benefit is limited.

E.g. If one bring an action alleging that the rent or profit of a certain house tenanted by another is limited in his favour, this action is not heard merely on the ground that the vaqf is limited in favour of that person if the Mutevelli of the vaqf is not the plaintiff.

But if the judge give leave to the beneficiary to sue and *Unless judge gives leave.* permit his suit. then the beneficiary also may bring or defend an action.

ART. 461.—In actions about philanthropic establishments limited and belonging to the public benefit, one of *One of the public may be a litigant in case of public vaqf.* the public can sue (Mejellé, 1644).

K

CHAPTER XIX.
Evidence relating to vaqfs.
SECTION I.
What evidence is admissible.

Evidence of
beneficiary in
favour of vaqf
admissible, in
an an action
about the vaqf
property.

ART. 462.—The evidence of a beneficiary in favour of a vaqf is admissible in a matter relating to the dedicated property itself.

E.g. If the Mutevelli of money made vaqf brings an action against someone who owes a fixed sum of money out of the capital monies of the vaqf, the evidence of the beneficiaries of that vaqf in favour of the Mutevelli is admissible.

Again if the Mutevelli of a vaqf bring an action against the possessor of a property, alleging that it is part of the Mustaghelat of the vaqf, but the possessor of the property defends the action and alleges that the property is his private property, the evidence of the beneficiaries of the vaqf in favour of the Mutevelli is admissible.

ART. 463.—If in a case in which in an action about a vaqf the Mutevelli is required to produce witnesses, he says he has no witnesses and afterwards produces some, these are received (*see* Art. 334).

Evidence of
beneficiary not
admissible in
action for
income.

ART. 464.—The evidence of a beneficiary in favour of the vaqf when it is a question about the interest or income due to the vaqf is not admissible.

E.g. If the Mutevelli of vaqf money bring an action against someone, alleging that he has to receive a fixed sum of money as interest of money which he lent to him out of the vaqf monies, and the defendant disputes the claim, the evidence of the beneficiaries of the dedication in favour of the Mutevelli is not admissible.

Again, if the Mutevelli of a vaqf brings an action against someone, alleging that he had let to him such a property out of the vaqf properties, and that he has to receive from him on account of deferred rent (Muejele) a fixed sum of money, and the person sued disputes the claim, the evidence of the beneficiaries of that vaqf in favour of the Mutevelli is not admissible.

As to ancient
vaqf.

ART. 465.—The evidence of witnesses that a place is ancient vaqf is admissible, although they do not mention the name of the dedicator.

Evidence of
descent.

ART. 466.—Witnesses deposing that a person is a descendant of the dedicator ought to declare the bonds of relationship existing between him and the dedicator.

Consequently, the evidence of witnesses declaring absolutely that someone is a descendant of the dedicator is not admissible if they do not declare the ties of relationship between them.

But when the plaintiff asserts that he is the descendant or relation of someone, who is proved to be a descendant of the dedicator and witnesses depose agreeably to this allegation, this evidence is considered sufficient, and there is no need to prove the ties of relationship between the plaintiff and the dedicator (*see* Art. 423).

ART. 467.—The decision of a judge in favour of himself about vaqf property or its income of which the benefit is appointed for himself is not to be executed. _{Beneficiary cannot be judge.}

E.g. If the Mutevelli of a vaqf, the income of which is dedicated for the benefit of the judge of a certain city, bring an action before the judge, alleging that a property possessed by someone as pure mulk and situated in that city is part of the Mustaghelat of that vaqf, and when the person sued denies the truth of his allegation, proves his claim by witnesses, the decision in respect of this given by that judge is not to be carried into execution.

The trial of such cases is taken before another judge to whom is committed the trial in that city of such vaqf cases, if there is such a judge, but if there is no such judge, the procedure required by Article 1908 of the Mejellé is followed.

N.B.—Many of these sections would not now be in force in Cyprus Courts other than the Sheri' Courts.

SECTION II.

Hearsay Evidence.

ART. 468.—Hearsay evidence about the corpus (asl vaqf) is admissible, if the ownership of the possessor is not based on some ground regarded by law as a means of ownership. _{About original vaqf.}

In this matter, by " asl vaqf " is meant the things relating to the dedication, on which the validity of the dedication depends.

E.g. If the Mutevelli of a vaqf brings an action about a property possessed by someone, alleging that it is the property of the vaqf, and the person sued alleges that that property is his absolute mulk without shewing the reason of his ownership and so disputes the claim of the Mutevelli, without declaring any reason regarded as a means of acquiring ownership, the hearsay evidence of persons deposing in favour of the claim of the Mutevelli is admissible.

But if the ownership of the possessor is based on a ground regarded in law as a means of acquiring ownership, such as purchase, gift and inheritance, then hearsay evidence about the original dedication is not admissible, but the proof of the judicial sanction (tesjil vaqf) is required and, in respect of that, hearsay evidence is not admissible.

E.g. If someone has bought a property from another and possesses it as pure mulk, and the Mutevelli of a vaqf brings an action, alleging that that property belongs to the Musta-ghelat of that vaqf, hearsay evidence in support of the Mutevelli's claim is not admissible.

Terms of the dedication.

ART. 469.—Hearsay evidence which relates only to the terms of the dedication is not admissible.

E.g. If one of the descendants of the dedicator bring an action, alleging that the dedicator directed that the income of a property, held as dedicated for the benefit of a certain object, should be applied for the benefit of his children and their descendants, hearsay evidence in support of the plaintiff's claim is not admissible.

Hearsay evidence about the terms of the dedication is admissible however, when on the defendant denying that a place is original vaqf, the witnesses who give hearsay evidence about its being original vaqf give evidence also about its terms.

SECTION III.

Preference of proof (Mejellé, 1756) (see note to Article 470 in Appendix).

Evidence of health.

ART. 470.—Evidence of health is preferred to that of mortal sickness.

E.g. If, after someone has dedicated a mulk property of his, and put the Mutevelli in possession, and obtained the judicial decision that the property is irrevocably dedicated, he dies, and his heirs bring an action alleging that he dedicated that property when he was in a state of mortal sickness, but the Mutevelli defends the action and says that the act of dedication was made when the dedicator was in good health, and both the litigants bring evidence of their allegations, the evidence of the Mutevelli is preferred.

Again, if someone has no heirs at all entitled to inherit, and after he has granted to another, with the leave of the Mutevelli, an Ijaretein vaqf in his possession, he dies, and the Mutevelli brings an action, alleging that the grantor made a grant of that property during the time of his mortal illness, and that on this account the grant is invalid, and that the property as Mahlul belongs to the vaqf but the grantee alleges that the grant was made when the grantor was in a state of health, and that consequently it is valid, the evidence of the grantee is preferred, if both the litigants are willing to bring evidence in support of their allegation.

Building on vaqf land.

ART. 471.—If, after someone has erected at his own expense a building on a vaqf site possessed by him at a rent, the Mutevelli brings an action alleging that the defendant erected the building by his order on the condition that he should bring the expense into account against the rent, but the defendant asserts that he erected it for himself, if both parties are willing to call evidence, the evidence of the Mutevelli is preferred.

ART. 472.—The proof of a particular thing is preferred to proof of a general thing (Mejellé, Art. 64).

That is to say, when the children of the first generation of the dedicator are the possessors of the income of a vaqf, if the children of the second generation of the dedicator bring an action alleging that the income of that vaqf had been appointed in favour of the descendants of the dedicator generally, and the children of the first generation of the dedicator allege that the income was dedicated in favour of the children and descendants of the dedicator from generation to generation, if both parties are willing to bring evidence in support of their contention the evidence of the children of the first generation is preferred.

The same thing applies to the Mutevelliship.

ART. 473.—If the Mutevelli of a vaqf contends that certain lands, situated at a place belong to the vaqf, whilst the land authorities allege that they are Arazi mirié, if they both wish to prove their contention, the evidence of the person who relies on common talk is preferred.

That is to say, if there is a common talk that the lands are vaqf, the evidence of the Mutevelli is preferred.

On the other hand if the common talk is that the lands are Arazi mirié then the evidence of the land authorities is preferred.

There being no common talk in favour of anyone the following rules will be observed.

If the lands are in the possession of the vaqf the evidence of the land authorities is preferred because he is not the possessor (Mejellé, Art. 1757).

But if they are possessed by the Beit-ul-mal then the evidence of the Mutevelli who is not the possessor is preferred.

ART. 474.—An action, the subject matter of which is a vaqf property, is looked upon as an action for unconditional ownership.

Consequently if each of the Mutevellis of two vaqfs alleges that a certain place belongs to the vaqf of which he is the Mutevelli and one of them is in possession of it, the evidence of the one who is not in possession is preferred (Mejellé, Art. 1757).

Also if someone claims the unconditional ownership of a place, without fixing the time when his right first arose, and the Mutevelli of a vaqf alleges that such place is vaqf, the evidence of the person not in possession is preferred, if one is in possession and the other is not.

That is to say, if such place is in possession of the person claiming the unconditional ownership, the evidence of the Mutevelli is preferred.

But if it is in possession of the Mutevelli the evidence of the person claiming the unconditional ownership, is preferred.

Ownership from fixed date.

ART. 475.—In an action about ownership acquired at a fixed date, the evidence of the person claiming the ownership from the earlier date is preferred (Mejellé, Art. 1760).

That is to say, if each of the Mutevelli's of two vaqfs alleges that a certain place belong to the vaqf for which he is Mutevelli and they both fix the date when the right of ownership first arose and the date fixed by one of them is prior to that fixed by the other, the evidence of the Mutevelli relying on the earlier date is preferred.

CHAPTER XX.

Circumstances under which the Mutevelli is required to take an oath and vice versa.

When Mutevelli called in to take an oath.

ART. 476.—In an action regarding a vaqf, the Mutevelli of such vaqf is not called upon to take an oath unless he be a party to the contract sued upon (Mejellé, Art. 1748).

E.g. If a person brings an action and alleges that a vaqf property in the possession of the Mutevelli is his mulk property and fails to prove his contention he is not entitled to call upon the Mutevelli to take an oath.

Also, if the Mutevelli of vaqf money brings an action against someone claiming a fixed sum of money due for money lent by his predecessor, and the defendant denies the claim setting up as a defence that he paid the amount in full to the predecessor while he was in office, and fails to prove his allegation, he cannot call upon the Mutevelli at the time being to deny it on oath.

Also, if, after someone has admitted that he owes a fixed sum of money to such a vaqf, he afterwards retracts his admission and alleges that he does not owe so much and that his admission was false, he cannot call upon the Mutevelli to swear that his admission was not false.

But a Mutevelli who is a party to a contract is liable to take an oath.

E.g. If someone alleges that he has let to the Mutevelli for a limited term, a Mustaghelat vaqf, which is in the possession of the Mutevelli, and the Mutevelli denies; if such person brings an action claiming delivery of the property he can, in case he fails to prove his contention, call upon the Mutevelli to state on oath that he did not let such property to him.

In the same way, if someone alleges that the Mutevelli of a vaqf has bought from him and receive delivery of certain things for the necessities of the vaqf, and brings an action claiming the purchase money, and the Mutevelli denies the claim, and the claimant fails to prove his contention, in such a case he can call upon the Mutevelli to deny it on oath.

Also when a Mutevelli brings an action against the lessee of a vaqf property claiming rent, due in arrears, and the lessee alleges that he has paid in full and delivered such rent to the Mutevelli and that he owes nothing, and the Mutevelli denies that he has received the money, and denies the truth of the defence, and the lessee fails to prove his contention, such lessee is entitled to call upon the Mutevelli to take an oath.

ART. 477.— A judge can call upon a Mutevelli who is guilty to take an oath as to whether he has committed any breach of trust against the vaqf without referring to a specific instance.

CHAPTER XXI.
Admission.

ART. 478.— No admission of a Mutevelli against a vaqf is allowed.

Admission of Mutevelli does not bind the vaqf.

E.g. If someone brings an action in respect of vaqf property possessed by a Mutevelli alleging that it is his mulk property and the Mutevelli admits and acknowledges the plaintiff's claim, the admission of the Mutevelli is not binding on the vaqf.

Consequently, an admission of this nature is not a ground for a decision against the vaqf.

ART. 479.— If someone says that a property possessed by him is vaqf, his word is taken to refer to an admission that such property had previously been made vaqf, and not as a dedication made at the time. Consequently the terms of dedication need not be included in the admission (Mejellé, 1628).

That property is vaqf.

ART. 480.— If someone, in whose favour the income, occupation or Mutevelliship of a vaqf is limited, admits that someone else, who is not proved to be one of the beneficiaries, is also one of the beneficiaries, his admission is given effect to so far as he is concerned, but not as regards his co-beneficiaries, if any (Mejellé, Art. 78).

Consequently, the person in whose favour the admission is made becomes a co-beneficiary so far as regards the share

Admission of beneficiary.

of the person making the admission and not as regards the shares of the others if any. After the death of a person having so made an admission, his admission ceases to be in force.

Consequently, his children are not bound by the admission of the deceased.

ART. 481.—An admission made by an Ijaretein tenant against a vaqf in respect of the ownership (raqabe) of an Ijaretein property is not valid.

E.g. If someone brings an action claiming the ownership of an Ijaretein Mustaghelat vaqf held by another, and the defendant admits that that property belongs to the plaintiff his admission is not given effect to or binding on the vaqf.

Consequently, if a judge decides that that property is the plaintiff's, basing his decision upon an admission of this kind, his decision is not valid.

Also if the Mutevelli of a vaqf bring an action alleging that an Ijaretein Mustaghelat property of another vaqf belongs to the vaqf for which he is Mutevelli and the defendant admits the action, his admission is not valid nor is effect given to it.

Admission by debtor.

ART. 482.—If the Mutevelli of dedicated money bring an action against someone, claiming a sum of money, which he alleges had been lent to him by his predecessor out of the estate of the vaqf for which he is Mutevelli, and the defendant denies the claim, but promises at the same time to pay the amount claimed if the former Mutevelli appears and states that he lent him the money, if afterwards the ex-Mutevelli appears and states that he lent him so many piastres, and the defendant does not admit that statement, he is not looked upon as having admitted that the amount is due by his mere promise.

In such a case if a judge, basing his decision on the mere promise, adjudge the defendant to pay the amount claimed, his decision is invalid.

But if the defendant admits the statement of the ex-Mutevelli, then he is adjudged to pay the sum claimed on the ground that he has admitted the same.

APPENDIX.

NOTES BY OMER HILMI.

ART. 15.—Mustaghel is general and Mussaqaf particular. But generally it is called Mussaqafat and Mustaghelat Mevqufe and thus Mustaghelat is used as the opposite of Mussaqafat.

Therefore according to the maxim, "when something general is mentioned as the opposite of a particular thing, from the general term is intended everything other than the particular thing," from the term Mustaghelat is meant vaqfs which are not Mussaqafat.

In different places in this book it is so used and intended.

ART. 33.—There is another kind of Evqaf-i-Mazbuta which, whilst their tevliets are in charge of persons to whom they were assigned by the dedication, are administered directly by the Imperial Ministry of Evqaf, and the Mutevellis are given a fixed salary and are not allowed to interfere with the affairs of the vaqfs.

This kind is called "Idaresi Mazbuta Evqaf." Like the vaqfs of Kyproulou, Jegalzadeler, and Shehid Mehmed Pasha.

To take the administration of vaqfs in this way is not in accordance with the Sheri' law.

ART. 63.—Because a subsequent assent is like a preceding vekalet. Because a person who holds property by Ijaretein, does not own its reqabe, but only the benefit to be derived from the vaqf property held by him.

ART. 111.—There is general consent that vaqfs are admissible but there is a difference of opinion between the Mujtehids as to when it is irrevocable or when it is not so.

According to the opinion of Imam Abu Hanife, vaqf is a revocable agreement like a loan; according to Imam Mohammed, vaqf is irrevocable on condition that delivery has been made to the Mutevelli; according to Imam Abu Youssuf vaqf is without any condition irrevocable.

According to the opinion of Imam Abu Hanife, if a person dedicates a property and even hands it over to the Mutevelli, the property dedicated does not cease to be the property of the dedicator and therefore the dedicator can revoke the dedication and possess the property dedicated in every way as possessor, and upon the death of the dedicator the heirs are entitled to the same rights.

According to the opinion of the Imam Mohammed any vaqf not handed over to the Mutevelli can be revoked.

According to the opinion of Imam Abu Youssuf simply by the dedicator saying "I have dedicated," the property dedicated ceases to be the property of the dedicator, and therefore he cannot revoke it.

Where there is a difference of opinion between the Mujtehids on a matter relating to a rule and the Qadi prefers the opinion of one of the Mujtehids and gives judgment according to it, the difference becomes of no importance, because there is a general agreement that the decision of Qadi is to be enforced in such a case.

Therefore when in a matter relating to a vaqf the Qadi prefers the opinion of one Mujtehid, in whose opinion a vaqf is irrevocable, and gives his judgment accordingly, that vaqf becomes irrevocable as all Mujtehids agree. Another Qadi cannot after that elect to follow the opinion of another Mujtehid and cancel the vaqf. That vaqf becomes irrevocable. This is what " tesjil " means.

Note to Art. 111 *by revisers.*—Mujtehid. A Mujtehid is a man whose views of the law are followed like those of jurisconsults in Rome.

There are various degrees of Mujtehid. The four principal are Hanefi, Shafiit, Malekit and Hambelit, the founders of the four branches of Moslems of the Sunni persuasion.

Of these the Hanefi school gives the more elastic interpretation of the law and is the one followed by the more civilized Moslem powers.

The principal Mujtehids of this school are Abou Hanifa also called the great Imam and his two pupils, Imam Mohammed and Imam Abou Youssuf.

Note to Art. 137 *by revisers.*—The second and third kinds of Takhsisat vaqfs are like mulk subject to the conditions of the dedicator (Khalis Eshref note to Art. 4 of the Land Code).

ART. 171.—What is meant by Defter Khaqani are the books which were prepared and written some 350 years ago through reliable recorders who were chosen and appointed from the Ulemas and officers of State.

All villages, cultivated lands, meras, forests, yaylak, kishlaks and all other lands in the dominion of his Imperial Majesty and their ownership were with great care enquired into, and these were recorded in those books in a manner free from doubt. When each book was finished it was submitted and signed by him at the top and approved and the Imperial Cypher put on it.

These books are kept in the special Record Office in the Imperial Office of Defter Khane according to the practice and usages established by the State when they were fresh introduced.

As these books were kept so properly and carefully in the manner above mentioned, the records in them remain free from suspicion ; no one can add anything to them.

The records of these books are agreed by all the later jurisconsults to be free from doubt, and they allowed judgment to be given on their contents without further proof (Mejellé, Art. 1737).

ART. 188.—This which is called " intiqal," is based on custom and usage and not upon the Sheri' ; therefore it is called customary intiqal (succession), because when the holder by Ijaretein dies, the contract of lease comes to an end according to the Sheri' law, and the tasarruf of the property held does not pass to his legal heirs.

ART. 224.—There is a difference of opinion among the jurisconsults about the lawfulness of taking something as price for the alienation of vaqf mussaqafat and mustaghellat held in Ijaretein.

In ancient ages the opinion of those jurisconsults who disallowed taking a price was acted upon, and actions for price were not heard by the judges. But lately the benefits of the people and the necessities of the age have been taken into consideration, and the second opinion *i.e.*, the validity of recovering a price in alienation, has been preferred and an Imperial Irade has been issued to this effect upon a report submitted by the Sheykh-ul-Islam. Therefore all judges in His Imperial Majesty's dominions are ordered to give judgment according to the second opinion. Any judgment given in accordance with the first opinion is of no force.

ART. 275.—It is explained in Art. 38 of the Evqaf Regulations dated 19 Jemazial-Akhir, 1280, that conversion of vahidelu vaqf property into Ijareteinlu without the sanction of the Sheri‘ and an Imperial Irade, should not be accepted by the Treasury of Evqaf, nor should it regard any seal or consent. Any one who makes such conversion is to be imprisoned from three months to two years or banished from six months to three years.

ART. 286.—Muqata‘a is fixed at the rate of 10 per thousand annually upon the registered value of the place.

This is levied in order to compensate the Evqaf Treasury as vaqf transactions such as sale, inheritance, and mahlul are no longer carried out in respect of an Ijareteinlu vaqf place converted into a public institution (*see* Imperial Irade dated 16 Ramazan, 1296.)

E.g. For a place thus converted into a public institution of which the registered value is 50,000 piastres an annual muqata‘a of 500 piastres is fixed.

Note to Art. 303 *by revisers.*—" Long distance." The term in Turkish is " muddet-i-sefer " which is explained in the Mejellé, Art. 1664 to mean " a distance from place to place of three days at a moderate rate of travelling, that is to say eighteen hours."

ART. 416.—It is forbidden to the judges to carry out the exchange of a vaqf property without first submitting the matter to the Sultan (*see* Imperial Firman dated A.H. 951).

Note to Art. 470 *by revisers.*—To understand the meaning of the term " preference of truths " it is necessary to know the procedure in the Sheri‘ Court.

Ordinarily evidence for the plaintiff only is allowed to be given. If the plaintiff produces the number of witnesses required by the law, and on enquiry the Court is satisfied that the witnesses are trustworthy, judgment is given in his favour.

The defendant cannot call evidence of a negative nature unless the evidence amounts to general knowledge.

But the defendant may put forward a claim which is inconsistent with the plaintiff's claim, *e.g.* if the plaintiff claims to be sole owner, the defendant claims to be joint owner with the plaintiff. In such a case only one side is allowed to call witnesses. The determination as to which party shall call evidence in such a case is called " Preference of Proofs."

INDEX.

	PAGE	ARTICLE
Abandonment by beneficiary	42	174
,, ,, Mutevelli	42	174
Acceptance of dedication—*See* Dedication, Refusal, Acceptance		
Accounts of Mutevelli, directed to be examined if officials think fit	80	312
,, ,, , examined by Judge	81	308
,, ,, , expenditure not sanctioned by dedicator not allowed	84	332
,, ,, , payment of grant out of principal	91	362
,, ,, , preceding Mutevelli	80	311
,, ,, , proof of claim	86	339
,, ,, , proof of expenditure	86	339
,, ,, , re-opening	80	310
,, ,, , unusual expenditure not allowed	84	333
Actions relating to vaqfs	103	421
Additions to vaqf property by beneficiary	100	409
Adi, meaning of	5	42
Admission by beneficiary	119	480
,, ,, debtor	120	482
,, ,, Mutevelli does not bind vaqf	119	478
,, estoppel by	105, 106	427—433
,, Mutevelli cannot make against vaqf	110, 111	445
,, that property is vaqf, meaning of	119	479
Advances by Mutevelli	88	348
,, of grants for beneficiaries, when recoverable by Mutevelli	88	348
Agent, Mutevelli may appoint	83	329
,, to buy, powers of	67, 68	258, 262
,, to sell, powers of	67, 68	256,257,261
,, revocation of authority	67, 68	259, 260
Agreement—*See* Alienation, agreement for.		
Ahfad, means grandchildren	3	22
Alien may make property vaqf	8	56
Alienation, agreement for, penalty on breach not enforceable	54	208
,, ,, ,, , without consent of Mutevelli not enforceable	54	206
,, by guardians of persons under disability	56	214
,, by sick person	54	209
,, conditional	57	218
,, condition to maintain alienor	57	219
,, consent required	52	199
,, defective	57	218
,, during mortal illness—*See* Mortal illness.		
,, of Ijaretein before a Judge	54	206
,, of Mussaqafat and Mustaghelat Vaqfs, what it is	3	17
,, of undivided share of Ijaretein Vaqf	63	240
,, of part of an Ijaretein Vaqf	63	238
,, option to rescind	58	220
,, price, recovery of	59	223
,, to guardians of persons under disability	56	216
Alienor, must be of age	53	203
,, ,, ,, sound mind	53	203
Alteration of dedication	38	161
,, ,, during last illness when power reserved	38	162
,, Mussaqafat	69	267
,, Takhsisat dedications	39	166
Appointment—*See* Mutevelli.		
Appointments—*See* Offices.		
Apportionment	92	366
Arrears of grants, when payable out of subsequent income	90	359

	PAGE	ARTICLE
Arazi Mirié granted as Mulk may be made Sahiha Vaqf	28	127
,, grant as Mulk, proof of	29	135
,, how validly granted as Mulk	28	128
,, made Mulk and dedicated tithe still payable	31	139
,, Mutevelli must not purchase	83	330
Arrears not payable out of income of subsequent year	90	359
Avariz Vaqfi, meaning of	5	36
Bailee, Mutevelli holds vaqf property as	85	337
Bankrupt—See Insolvent.		
Bedeli Feragh is the price for alienation	3	17
Beneficiaries, Murteziqa and Ehli Vazaif	3	21
Beneficiaries take in equal shares unless contrary provision	34	149
Beneficiary, abandoning office does not lose right	42	174
,, , additions to vaqf property by	100	409, 410
,, , cannot be Judge	115	467
,, , dedicator should name a lasting object	15	80
,, , description of	31, 32	140, 141
,, , failure of	14	77
,, , ,, , income spent on poor	15	79
,, , joint, trespass by	100	408
,, , may be a class in general	14	76
,, , must be an object of reverence in itself	14	74
,, , must be an object of reverence to dedicator	14	74
,, , must be clearly defined	12, 13	69, 70, 71
,, , must be within the terms of the dedication	43	175
,, , need not be declared	14	75
,, , need not be of same religion as dedicator	8	57
,, , non-existing at time of dedication	14	77
,, , of a vaqf is called Meshrutun leh, Mevqufun aleih and Masraf-i-Vaqf	1	7
,, , option to Mutevelli is valid	13	71
,, , poor, descendants of dedicator preferred	44	180
,, , quarter, Mussulman and non-Mussulman share alike	44	181
,, , rejecting benefit at time of dedication is deprived of his right	42	174
,, , to be selected by Mutevelli, valid	13	71
,, , unknown, income given to the poor, on Judge's decision	40	169
,, , vacant vaqf of, poor is	15	79
,, , village, Mussulman and non-Mussulman share alike	44	181
,, , who may be, children of dedicator	17	89
,, , ,, ,, , dedicator may be	17	89
,, , ,, ,, , infant may be	8	53(2)
,, , ,, ,, , lunatic may be	8	53(2)
,, , ,, ,, , person in second childhood	8	53(2)
,, , with exclusive right to inhabit can let	99	404
,, , with right to income cannot inhabit	97	395
,, , with right to inhabit cannot let	97	394
Benefit cannot be taken by person outside the dedication	43	175
,, of property, dedication of, sometimes construed as dedication of thing itself	9	60
,, of property without the property cannot be made vaqf	9	60
Bequest of unrecovered debt for vaqf is valid	9	60
,, to be made vaqf must not exceed one third of the estate	9	60
Borrowing powers of the Mutevelli	87, 89	345—349
Boundaries of property need not be declared in dedication	12	66
Breach of terms of dedication for benefit	39	165
,, ,, ,, ,, necessity	39	165
Building by Ijaretein tenant does not belong to vaqf	70	268
,, ,, Mutevelli on vaqf land	101	414
,, liable to be pulled down cannot be made vaqf	13	72
,, Muqata'a vaqf—See Muqata'a.		
,, on Mulk site if dedicated cannot be dedicated alone	16	85

	PAGE	ARTICLE
Building on vaqf land by person other than Mutevelli ..	102	415
„ „ „ site for vaqf is irrevocably vaqf	27	123
„ passes in dedication of site	18	95
„ wrongful by tenant	70	268
Buying with intention to dedicate is not a dedication	7	54
Cemetery, an undivided share cannot be dedicated for	11	64
„ , dedication for, irrevocable after burial	24	114
Change—*See* Alteration.		
Charitable institution, useless and received income how spent ..	87	343
„ „ —*See* Pious establishments.		
Children—*See* Interpretation.		
Chose in action, as to dedication of	9	60
Claim by Mutevelli, proof of	86	339
Collateral document, qualification of, grant by	104, 105	425—428
Common establishments, no prescription	111	449
Co-Mutevellis, office of joint	82	327
Compromise of actions by Mutevelli	84	334
Conditional alienation	56	214
„ dedication	12	68
Condition uncertain, what is	12	67
„ subsequent to sale of Ijareteinlu cannot be enforced	53	201
Consent of dedicator to dedication is required	8	54(2)
„ heirs must be after death of dedicator	20	102
„ Mutevelli necessary for alienation of Ijareteinlu ..	52, 53	199
„ „ required for exchange when vaqfs different	54	205
Consequences of dedication	7	50
„ „ „ dedicator loses all rights over the pro-		
perty	26	119
„ „ „ „ not bound to give other pro-		
perty if vaqf evicted ..	26	120
„ „ „ heirs of dedicator do not inherit ..	26	119
Construction, benefit sometimes construed to mean property ..	9, 10	60
„ , boundaries described overrule inconsistent de-		
scription	19	97
„ , change of vaqf means change of terms	38	164
„ , dedication of a building site includes buildings,		
trees and vines on it	18	95
„ , dedication of a property includes rights attached		
to it..	18	94
„ , dedication unqualified gives income, not right to		
inhabit	43	176
„ , division equal if no direction	43	177
„ , division in equal shares implied	34, 35	149
„ , false description of quantity	19	98
„ , interpretation—*See* Interpretation.		
„ , pronoun refers to nearest noun	34	148
Contribution for repairs when given	64	242
Conversion of dedicated property	18	90
Co-owner, contribution for repairs as to	64	242
„ , of Ijaretein Vaqf when right to pre-emption.. ..	63, 64	240
Court, alienation before	54	206
Creation of vaqf	6	44
Custody of money by Mutevelli	83, 84	331
Custom followed where intention of dedicator unknown ..	40	168
Cyprus Law, disabilities of heirs, Act XX. of 1895.		
„ „ Ijaretein Vaqf, inheritance of non-Mussulman, Act XX. of 1895.		

	PAGE	ARTICLE
Damages, wrongful appropriation ..	98	402
Death, proof of	49	191
,, simultaneous of relations ..	49, 50	192
Debt, direction to pay future, valid	17, 18	89
Debtor, in mortal sickness, dedication by..	19	99
,, —See Insolvent.		
Debts, interest runs while debt is unpaid ..	89	352
,, , payment of ..	89	355
,, unrecovered cannot be made vaqf except by bequest ..	9	60
,, —vaqf has no priority	89	354
Deceased Mutevelli, liability of his estate	85	338
,, person, vaqf has no preference over other creditors ..	89	354
Dedicated money	88	350
,, ,, —See Grants.		
,, ,, condition to maintain principal	91	361
,, ,, payment of grants out of principal, consequences of ..	91	362
,, ,, when income does not cover expenses ..	91	363
,, thing—See Vaqf.		
Dedication—See Takhsis.		
,, acceptance of, is final ..	7	49
,, ,, silence is	7	48
,, ,, when necessary	6	47
,, alteration of terms	38	161
,, ,, during last illness, where power reserved ..	38	162
,, beneficiaries—See Beneficiary.		
,, buying with intention to dedicate is not sufficient ..	7	54
,, by will, revocation how made	27	122
,, ,, ,, of ..	27	122
,, condition to re-invest, valid ..	13	70
,, consequence of ..	7	50
,, consequences of—See Consequences.		
,, construction—See Construction.		
,, custom followed when intention of dedicator, unknown	40	168
,, dumb person, by	6	45
,, force induced by, invalid	8	54(2)
,, for Mesjid with option reserved, option invalid ..	12, 13	69
,, how made, boundaries of property need not be stated	12	66
,, ,, ,, must not depend on uncertain condition	12	67
,, ,, ,, property known by mark or description	12	66
,, ,, ,, purchase by Mutevelli out of the income of the vaqf is not ..	7	55
,, ,, ,, purchase by Mutevelli with the thing dedicated is	7	55
,, ,, ,, to take effect in the future not valid ..	12	68
,, ,, ,, to take effect on death may operate as bequest ..	12	68
,, invalid if beneficiary not clearly determined ..	12, 13	69
,, ,, induced by force	8	54 (2)
,, irrevocable—See Irrevocability.		
,, means vaqf	1	1
,, mistake in Vaqfieh	41	172
,, mortal sickness, by person in—See Mortal sickness.		
,, motive of	7	52
,, option reserved with, generally invalid ..	12, 13	69
,, perpetual, must be ..	13	70
,, refusal of, is final	7	49
,, ,, to accept, effect of	7	49
,, revocable—See Irrevocability.		
,, revokes prior, will	17	87
,, Sahiha, terms and conditions of, must be complied with	39	165
,, ,, ,, , breach of, in cases of necessity ..	39	165
,, Takhsisat, alteration of	39	166
,, temporary invalid ..	13	70
,, terms of Vaqfieh not carried out unless it has been proved and acted upon ..	40	170

	PAGE	ARTICLE
Dedication terms breach of, for benefit of vaqf	39	165
„ „ inconsistent	42	173
„ „ interpretation—See Interpretation.		
„ „ invalid if contrary to Sacred Law	40	167
„ „ of	6	44
„ „ „ when Vaqfieh differs from document in Defter Khaqani	40	171
„ thing dedicated must be lawful for use	6	46
„ „ „ possession must have been acquired	6	46
„ „ „ what may be	6	43
„ to take effect in the future not valid	12	68
„ „ „ on death invalid	17	86
„ „ „ may operate as bequest	12, 17	68, 86
„ unqualified gives income, not right to inhabit	43	176
„ validity. By writing alone, not valid	17	88
„ „ direction to pay future debt of dedicator, valid	17, 18	89
„ „ must be made known and attested	17	88
„ „ power of exchange, valid	18	90
„ „ to sell and distribute, price invalid	18	90
„ what may be dedicated—See Vaqf.		
„ „ most acceptable	7	53
„ who can make, non-Mussulman can	8	56
„ „ may make, infants cannot	8	53 (2)
„ „ „ by lunatics, invalid	8	53 (2)
„ „ „ „ by persons in second childhood invalid	8	53 (2)
„ „ „ „ not free, invalid	8	53 (2)
„ „ „ „ inhibited person cannot	8	55 (2)
„ „ „ „ must be capable of doing acts of charity	8	53 (2)
„ „ „ „ „ transferring ownership	8	53 (2)
„ „ „ „ slave may with master's permission	8	53 (2)
„ „ „ „ —See Dedicator		
„ wife in favour of, until re-marriage	37	158
„ with condition to sell for dedicator in case of need, invalid	13	70
Dedicator, free, must be	7	51
„ full age, must be of	7	51
„ inability to dedicate proof	30	136
„ may be a non-Mussulman	8	56
„ must have legal capacity	6	43
„ must not be infant	8	53 (2)
„ „ „ inhibited	8	55 (2)
„ „ „ insolvent	25	117
„ „ „ second childhood, in	8	53 (2)
„ „ „ slave, unless he has master's permission	8	53 (2)
„ need not be subject of a Mahomedan country	8	56
„ need not be of same religion as beneficiaries	8	57
„ sound mind of, must be	7	51
Defect, option to rescind for	58	220
Defective alienation	57	218
Delegation of office	79, 94	306, 380
Descendants of dedicator preferred to other poor	44	180
Descent, proof of	103, 104	422, 423
Destruction of vaqf property	100	407
Devise—See Will.		
Difference of religion when a bar to inheritance	50	193
Direction to pay future debt of dedicator, valid	17, 18	89
Discretionary vaqfs	13	71
Dismissal of Mutevelli	81	317
Division equal if no direction	43	177
„ in equal shares implied	34, 35	149
„ of benefit of Ijaretein Vaqf—prior occupation does not count	63	236
„ „ „ „ revocable, unless Mutevelli consents	63	237

L

		PAGE	ARTICLE
Division of benefit of Ijaretein Vaqf—when allowed		62	235
,, of dedicated house not allowed		45	183
Ehli Vazaif—people who receive vazife		3	21
Escheat—*See* Mahlul.			
Establishments common, no prescription		111	449
Estate of deceased Mutevelli, liability of		85	338
Estoppel by admission		105, 106	427 431,433
,, by payment of rent		106	430
,, of lessee		106	429
,, of vendor		106	432
Eviction of vaqf by third party		26	120
Evidence, hearsay, when admissible		115, 116	468
,, whose admissible		114	462
Evlad-i-sulbieh means the direct issue of a person		3	23
Evqaf plural of Vaqf		1	2
Evqaf-i-Mazbuta—authority of Minister of Evqaf		4	33
,, ,, meaning of		4	33
,, ,, two categories of		4	33
,, Mulhaqa—authority of Minister of Evqaf		4	34
,, ,, meaning of		4	34
,, Mustesna, meaning of		4, 5	35
Excessive damage, rescission of partition for		61, 62	233
Excessive injury, option to rescind alienation for		58	221
Exchange of vaqf property, effect of		26	119
,, ,, ,, power to make is valid		18	90
,, ,, ,, what may be taken in exchange		102	417
,, ,, ,, when allowed		102	416
,, ,, ,, when irrevocable		103	420
Expenditure by Mutevelli, proof of		86	339
,, of money of one vaqf on another		86	340
,, of tenant on repairs		97	396
Failure of beneficiary		14, 15	77
,, ,, income spent on poor		15	79
False description of property dedicated		19	98
False representation invalidates appointment to tevliet		76	297
Faqir, meaning of		3	28
Farigh, means alienor		3	17
Feragh bil vefa, means mortgage		3	19
Feragh-i-qati' is an unconditional sale		3	18
Feragh, means alienation		3	17
Force invalidates dedication		8	54(2)
Fraud, option to rescind for		58, 59	222
Ghedik, meaning of		5	40
Ghalle-i-Vaqf, means the benefit of vaqf property		1	5
Gift of Ijareteinlu final after Mutevellis' consent		53	202
Gift of Mulk on Muqata'a site		73	280
Grandchildren are called Ahfad		3	22
Grant accrues daily		92	369
Grant, children born subsequently		92	370
,, condition to maintain principal		91	361
,, construction, " poor "		93	371
,, dismissed person entitled until dismissal made known		92	365
,, gift, as a		90	358
,, Mutevelli cannot recover sum paid as		92	367

		PAGE	ARTICLE
Grant, payment how made		91	360
,, ,, of, out of principal		91	362
,, qualification of, by collateral document		104, 105	425, 428
,, repairs take precedence of		101	411
,, two sorts		90	356
,, wage, as a		90	357
,, wages, increase of		91, 92	364
,, when income does not cover expenditure		91	363
,, when payable out of subsequent income		90, 91	359
Guardian cannot buy infant's property		56	216
,, under a will may exercise a power in his own favour		35	155
,, purchase of vaqf by, for c.t.q.		56	215
,, repairs of Ijaretein property, etc.		56, 57	217
,, sale by, of vaqf property for c.t.q.		56	214
Hearsay evidence when admissible		115	468
Heir, mortgagee can hold against		65	247
,, —See Inheritance.			
Heirs assent must be given after death of dedicator		20	102
Hiring on account of vaqf by Mutevelli		96	391
Homicide, when a bar to inheritance		51, 52	195
House dedicated, division of		45	183
Ijareteinlu, alienation of		52	198
,, ,, agreement for, not enforceable		54	207
,, ,, ,, ,, penalty on revocation not enforceable		54	208
,, ,, before a Judge		54	206
,, ,, complete though sened not prepared		53	200
,, ,, condition subsequent to sale of no force		53	201
,, ,, consent of Mutevelli required		52	199
,, ,, ,, required		53	201
,, ,, of part		63	238
,, ,, of undivided share		63, 64	240
,, alienor must be of age		53	203
,, ,, sound mind, must be of		53	203
,, building by tenant		70	268
,, cannot be dedicated		10	63
,, contribution for repairs, when given		64	242
,, co-owner no pre-emption by Sacred Law		64	241
,, ,, pre-emption, houses and dwellings in ,, respect of		64	241
,, division of benefit—See Division of benefit.			
,, exchange allowed		54	205
,, where vaqfs different, consent of Mutevellis required		54	205
,, gift final after Mutevelli's consent		53	202
,, grant by Mutevelli of unowned share		63	239
,, inheritance—See Death. Inheritance.			
,, ,, brother		48	190
,, ,, brothers and sisters by father or mother		48	190
,, ,, children of deceased children take the share of their father		47	190
,, ,, difference of nationality		51	194
,, ,, ,, of religion		50, 51	193
,, ,, great grandchildren no right		46	189
,, ,, homicide		51, 52	195
,, ,, husband		49	190
,, ,, Mahlul		52	197
,, ,, parents		47	190
,, ,, right of		45, 46	188
,, ,, sister		48	190

		PAGE	ARTICLE
Ijareteinlu, inheritance slavery		52	196
,, ,, wife		49	190
,, lessee not liable for Muejele		69	264
,, letting Ijare-i-Vahide Vaqf as		71	274
,, letting of		45	187
,, Mahlul grant of property as, by mistake		69	265
,, Mahlul when		50	192
,, meaning of		5	37
,, mortgage—*See* Mortgage of Ijaretein Vaqf.			
,, partition—*See* Partition			
,, Public Establishment, conversion into		74	286
,, right of tenant		45, 46	188
,, right of vaqf		45, 46	188
,, turned into Public Establishment should be made Muqata‘a		74	286
,, Vahide-i-Vaqf letting of, as		71	274
,, waste, liability of Ijaretein tenant for		69	263
,, wrongful building by tenant		70	268
Ijare-i-Vahidelu Evqaf, meaning of		5	38
,, Zemin, meaning of		5	39
Income condition to maintain principal		91	361
,, given by unqualified dedication		43	176
,, how paid		91	360
,, of useless charitable institutions, how spent		87	343
,, ,, Mesjid how dealt with		87	344
,, when insufficient for expenses		91	363
Inconsistent statement as to property dedicated		19	98
,, terms in Vaqfieh		42	173
Increase of wages		91, 92	364
Infant cannot alienate		53, 54	203
,, ,, dedicate		8	53(2)
Infants purchase by guardian—*See* Guardian.			
Inhabit, right to, not given by unqualified dedication		43	176
Inheritance, homicide when a bar		51, 52	195
,, nationality, difference of		51	194
,, of price on alienation		59	223
,, slavery a bar to		52	196
,, when barred by difference of religion		50	193
,, —*See* Ijareteinlu inheritance.			
Inhibited person cannot dedicate		8	55(2)
Insolvents dedication cannot be declared irrevocable		25	117
,, ,, good if made before insolvency		25	117
Intention to dedicate does not make dedication		7	54
Interest on debts runs till debt paid		89	352
Interpretation "children"		31, 32	140
,, "children and children's children from generation to generation"		32	142
,, ,, ,, children of children		32	141
,, ,, from generation to generation		33	145
,, ,, includes "child"		34	146
,, ,, of children includes children of daughters		35	150
,, ,, sometimes construed "grandchildren"		34	147
,, ,, twice		32	141
,, ,, unqualified includes children born after dedication		35	151
,, description words of		32	141
,, freed slaves		38	160
,, "male children of children" includes "male children of daughters"		35	150
,, "nearest"		36	156
,, "poor"		33	144
,, "poor neighbours"		37	159
,, "relations" does not include children and parents		35	153
,, ,, includes Mussulman and non-Mussulman		35, 36	154
,, —*See* Construction.			

	PAGE	ARTICLE
Invalidity of terms of dedication contrary to Sacred Law ..	40	167
Irrevocability benefit done to vaqf, irrevocable	27, 28	123
,, by decision of Judge after trial	23	111
,, by judgment upon trial after death of dedicator	23, 24	112
,, of dedication of cemetery	24	114
,, eviction of vaqf by third party	26	120
,, insolvent's dedication cannot be declared irrevocable	25	117
,, Mesjid dedication of	24	114
,, not established by decision of arbitrator.. ..	23	112
,, not in general established, except by judgment after trial, or dedication by will	23, 24	111, 114
,, property added to vaqf property require new decision	25	115
Issue direct called Evlad-i-Sulbieh..	3	23
,, ,, including grandchildren Nesl, Zurriyet	3	24
Istibdal means an exchange of vaqf for Mulk property	4	31
,, Tesjili, meaning of	4	32
Istiglal, meaning of	3	20
Interest runs while debt is unpaid	89	352
Jabi-i-Vaqf, meaning of	2	12
Joint beneficiary, trespass by	100	408
Judge alienation of Ijareteinlu, before	54	206
,, beneficiary cannot be	115	467
,, leave to be obtained before sale and re-investment ..	13	70
,, Mutevelli must obtain assent for acts beyond his authority	82	326
,, , power of, to give income to poor when beneficiary unknown	40	169
,, ,, to appoint Qaimaqam-i-Mutevelli	78	303
,, ,, to authorise breach of terms of dedication ..	39	165
Kharajié Arazi, made vaqf are Sahiha Vaqfs	28	125
,, ,, tax still payable after dedication	31	139
Land Law, when applicable to Takhsisat Vaqf	30	137
,, vaqf, different divisions of	43, 44	178
Lapse of ownership before dedication must be proved	30	136
Lapsed share by disability not Mahlul	52	197
Last illness, alteration of dedication under power, reserved ..	38	162
Lease of Ijare-i-Vahide Vaqf	70	270
,, ,, ,, ,, —See Letting.		
,, property under, effect of dedication..	9	60
,, ,, ,, may be made vaqf..	10	61
Leased Ijaretein Vaqf may be mortgaged..	65	246
Lessee, estoppel of	106	429
,, has no right to renewal of lease of Ijare-i-Vahide ..	71	273
,, of Ijaretein Vaqf not liable for Muejele	69	264
Letting Ijare-i-Vahide Vaqf at a Muqata'a rent	71	274
,, ,, ,, ,, at Ijaretein rent	71	275
,, ,, ,, ,, term of lease..	70	271
,, of vaqf, after letting higher offer not to be taken ..	97	393
,, ,, beneficiary may take	95	383
,, ,, ,, with right to income cannot prevent	97	395
,, ,, death of Mutevelli does not dissolve lease ..	96	386
,, ,, dissolution of contract	98	401
,, ,, excessively deficient rent, what is	96	398
,, ,, if rent prepaid, new Mutevelli cannot recover any	96	388
,, ,, increase of rent when value rises	97	393
,, ,, Mutevelli cannot claim rent from poor entitled to free habitations	98	400
,, ,, ,, let to a relation	95	385
,, ,, ,, ,, ,, to himself without leave of Judge	95	384

	PAGE	ARTICLE
Letting of Vaqf Mutevelli may let at a rack rent though dedicator directed a smaller rent	98	399
,, ,, new Mutevelli may recover rent..	96	387
,, ,, property dedicated to be inhabited cannot be let	97	394
,, ,, recovery of deficiency when rent too low ..	96	392
,, ,, rent must be equal to letting value	96	391
,, ,, rise in value of property course to be adopted	97	393
, ,, when lease defective, rack rent to be paid ..	97	397
,, ,, ,, ,, invalid, rack rent to be paid ..	98	398
Liability of estate of deceased Mutevelli	85	338
Loans by Mutevelli	83, 84	331
Loan succeding Mutevelli can recover	89	353
Lunatic cannot dedicate	8	53(2)
Lunatic's purchase and sale by guardain—See Guardian.		
Mahall-i-vaqf, meaning of	1	1
Mahlul, grant of property as, by mistake	69	265
,, mortgaged property becoming	65	248
,, shares lapsed through disability are not	52	197
Masraf-i-Vaqf, meaning of	1	7
Mazbuta Evqaf, meaning of	4	33
Mefrugh bih, meaning of	3	17
,, leh	3	17
Meremet-i-ghairi Mustehlike, meaning of	4	30
,, Mustehlike, meaning of	4	29
Meshrutun leh, meaning of	1	7
Mesjid, adding to	45	185
,, alteration of	18	93
,, an undivided share cannot be dedicated for	11	64
,, dedication for, by person in mortal sickness	22	109
,, when irrevocable	24	114
,, dedication of	17	92
,, enlargement of	45	185
,, income of useless how dealt with	87	343
,, rebuilding larger one	45	185
,, useless how dealt with	87	344
Mevat land acquired as Mulk when dedicated, is Sahiha Vaqf ..	28	126
Mevquf, means dedicated	1	1
Mevqufun aleih, meaning of	1	7
Mirié Arazi—See Arazi Mirié		
Mistake in Vaqfieh	41	172
Money dedicated	88	350
,, ,, condition to maintain principal	91	361
,, ,, —See Dedicated money, grants.		
,, given to Mutevelli to be expended on vaqf and spent cannot be recovered	27	123
,, of one vaqf, expenditure of on another	86	340
Mortal sickness, alienation of Mustaghelat during, when valid	54, 55	209
,, ,, alienation to heir during	55	211
,, ,, dedication by debtor in state of.. ..	19	99
,, ,, by person in state of, for heir for life and then to charity	22	108
,, ,, dedication by person in state of, for Mesjid ..	22	108
,, ,, ,, ,, ,, ,, in favour of heir	22	108
,, ,, ,, ,, ,, ,, who has heirs	20	101
,, ,, ,, ,, ,, ,, ,, a wife only	21	104
,, ,, ,, ,, ,, ,, ,, husband only..	21	105
,, ,, ,, ,, ,, ,, , no heirs	19	100
,, ,, judicial decision in time of, of previous dedication	22	110
,, ,, —See Sick person.		
,, ,, what is	21, 55	107, 211

	PAGE	ARTICLE
Mortgage of Ijaretein Vaqf, death of mortgagee does not make property Mahlul	66	253
,, ,, ,, destruction of property does not extinguish debt	66	249
,, ,, ,, lease by mortgagee to mortgagor	66,67	254
,, ,, ,, leased property	65	246
,, ,, ,, leave of Mutevelli required	65	244
,, ,, ,, Mahlul, when property becomes	65	248
,, ,, ,, mortgagee can hold against heir till payment	65	247
,, ,, ,, mortgagor has the benefit of the property	66	252
,, ,, ,, mortgagor pays Muejele	66	251
,, ,, ,, part, mortgage of	65	245
,, ,, ,, redemption of	65	244
,, ,, ,, redemption, stipulation against, invalid	66	250
,, power of sale	68	261
Mortgaged property, consequences of dedication	10	61
,, ,, dedicated, rule where dedicator dies before debt paid	10	61
,, ,, may be made vaqf	9	61
Moveable property, when may be made vaqf	9	59
Muajele gives to income of vaqf	70	269
Muejele not payable by lessee	69	264
,, payable by mortgagor	66	251
Muessesati Khairiye, meaning of	2	10
,, ,, —See Pious Establishments.		
Mulhaqa Evqaf, meaning of	4	34
Mulk, gift of, on Muqata‘a site	73	280
Munqati‘ el akhir, meaning of	15	78
,, evvel ,, ,,	15	77
,, wasat ,, ,,	15	79
Muqata‘a, letting Ijare-i-Vahide Vaqf at	71	274
,, meaning of	5	39
,, vaqf gift of mulk on	73	280
,, ,, ,, by guardian to infant	73	280
,, ,, grant of site, leave of Mutevelli required	73	279
,, ,, heirs of buildings, trees and vines takes land gratis	72	277
,, ,, Ijaretein Vaqf should be made Muqata‘a if turned into a Public Establishment	74	286
,, ,, inheritance	74	285
,, ,, land subject to buildings, trees and vines	72	277
,, ,, Mulk on, considered as moveable	74	284
,, ,, owner how long entitled	74	282
,, ,, partition of Mulk on	73	281
,, ,, ,, of site	73	281
,, ,, pre-emption, no right of, in respect of Mulk on	74	284
,, ,, rent may be raised	74	283
,, ,, sale of buildings, trees or vines, unless expressly excepted land passes	72	277
,, ,, sale of land, buildings, trees and vines do not pass	72	277
,, ,, vaqf does not take buildings, trees and vines belonging to tenant who dies	73	278
,, vaqfs, what they are	72	276
Murtezika, meaning of	3	21
Mussaqaf, meaning of	2	15
Mussaqafat Vaqf, alienation of, what it is	3	17
,, alteration of	69	267
,, plural of Mussaqaf	2	15
Mustaghel, meaning of	2	14
Mustaghelat, plural of Mustaghel	2	14
Mustaghelat Vaqf, alienation of, what it is	3	20
Mustesna Evqaf, meaning of	4, 5	35
Mutekellimun‘ ala el Vaqf, meaning of	2	9

		PAGE	ARTICLE
Mutevelli,	abandoning office does not lose right	42	174
,,	accounts—*See* Accounts.		
,,	acts before dismissal by Judge, are valid	81	318
,,	advances by	88	348
,,	advances for grants when recoverable	88	348
,,	agent, may appoint	83	329
,,	appointee only has right to be	75	291
,,	appointment obtained by false representation, invalid	76	297
,,	appointment of himself by guardian under will	36	155
,,	appointed to obtain judicial sanction	76	294
,,	bailee, holds as	85	337
,,	borrowing powers	87	345
,,	building on vaqf land by	101, 102	414
,,	cannot be Nazir	77	300
,,	cannot make admission against vaqf	110	445
,,	cannot recover a sum paid as a grant	92	367
,,	change of terms about, by dedicator allowed	38	163
,,	compromise of action by	84	334
,,	consent of, necessary for alienation of Ijareteinlu	53	202
,,	consent to exchange required where vaqfs different	54	205
,,	construction of appointment "Elder child of dedicator"	77	299
"	,, ,, 'the most competent children"	77	298
,,	custody of money	83, 84	331
,,	deceased, liability of estate	85	338
,,	dedicator is, if no one appointed	75	293
,,	dismissal, causes of	80	313
,,	,, for bad faith	80	308
,,	,, illegal charges must be proved	81	319
,,	,, from one vaqf, on, is dismissed from all	81	317
,,	executor of dedicator is, if none appointed	76	296
,,	grant of tevliet to another by	79	306
,,	,, of unowned share	63	239
,,	has no right to new vaqf by same dedicator	76	295
,,	hiring for vaqf by	96	389
,,	his consent makes gift of Ijareteinlu, final	53	202
,,	holds as bailee	85	337
,,	if more than one, all must assent	82	327
,,	infant, substitute appointed	75	288
,,	is also called Qaim-i-Vaqf and Mutekellimun'ala el Vaqf	2	9
,,	is designated by the Vaqfieh or appointed by the Judge	2	10
,,	joint Mutevellis	75, 82	290, 327
,,	Judge appoints on vacancy	75	292
,,	leave required for grant of Muqata'ali site	73	279
,,	,, ,, for mortgage	65	246
,,	liable if he appoints improper agent	83	329
,,	,, to repay grants out of principal	91	362
,,	liability for actions beyond powers	83, 84	331
,,	loans by	83, 84	331
,,	must be competent to direct vaqf	75	287
,,	,, ,, of age	75	287
,,	,, ,, of sound mind	75	287
,,	,, ,, trustworthy	75	287
,,	,, not purchase Arazi Mirié	83	330
,,	,, obtain assent of Nazir	83	328
,,	,, ,, leave of Judge for acts outside his authority	82	326
,,	meaning of	2	8
,,	no appointed, Judge appoints on death of dedicator	75	293
,,	of Ijaretein Vaqf can recover for waste	69	263
,,	pluralities	75	290
,,	power to sell material of ruined building	26	119
,,	power to root out dead trees and sell them	26	119
,,	Qaimaqam—*See* Qaimaqam-i-Mutevelli.		
,,	re-instalment of depraved	82	325
,,	release of part of debt by	85	336

	PAGE	ARTICLE
Mutevelli, resignation by	82	324
" sometimes called Nazir	78	302
" succeeding can sue for loan	89	353
" when appointment not clear, Judge decides	77	301
" " required to take an oath	118	476
" woman may be	75	289
Mutevelliship, decision of rival claim to vacant	78, 79	303
Nationality, difference of, when a bar to inheritance	51	194
Nazir, cannot be Mutevelli	77	300
" Mutevelli, is sometimes called	78	302
" " must obtain his consent	83	328
" Vaqf means overseer	2	11
Nesl, meaning of	3	24
Nizamli Gedikiati Mevquf, meaning of	5	42
" meaning of	5	41
Non-Mussulman may be a dedicator	8	57
Offices absence of appointee	95	382
" appointee must be a fit person	93	373
" " of the class directed	93	374
" death of appointee	94	375
" inconsistent appointments not allowed	94	375
" neglect of duties	95	381
" power of appointee to appoint proxy	94	380
" right to pay when proxy appointed	95	380
" transfer of appointment	94	376
" where Mutevelli has power to appoint and dismiss	94	378
Option reserved in dedication	12	69
" to Mutevelli to select beneficiary	13	71
" to rescind for defect	58	220
" " " excessive injury	58	221
" " " fraud	58, 59	222
" " " sale	58	220
Oral evidence, cannot vary written contract by	105	426
Ouster, return of price on	59, 60	225
Parole evidence inadmissible to contradict written grant	105	426
Part of Ijaretein Vaqf is alienable	63	236
Parties to actions, actions about Muqata'a Vaqf	112	451
" " " action about property of which rent or occupation dedicated	113	460
" " " about public vaqf	113	461
" " " by beneficiaries	112	457
" " " for damage for wrongful appropriation	112	456
" " " for ownership Mutevelli must be	111	450
" " " for possession (tasarruf) Mutevelli must be	111	450
" " " for price	112	454
" " " for rent	112	453
" " " for wrongful appropriation Mutevelli need not be	112	456
" " " to settle boundaries	112	455
" " " claim to Mutevelliship	113	458
" " " opposing claim to vacant tevliet	113	459
Parties to action, where more than one vaqf concerned, all Mutevellis must be present	112	451
Partition of Ijaretein Vaqf, enforced	60, 61	229
" " " equalization by payment	62	234
" " " guardian by	61	230

	PAGE	ARTICLE
Partition of Idjaretein Vaqf properties cannot be joined compulsorily	61	232
,, ,, ,, property ghediks when there are	61	231
,, ,, ,, when allowed	60	227
,, Mulk on Muqata'a site	73	281
,, Muqata'a site	73	281
,, rescinded for excessive damage	61, 62	233
Payment of debts	89	355
,, of grant, how made	91	360
Penalty on revocation of agreement to alienate not enforceable	54	208
Person in second childhood cannot dedicate	8	53(2)
Pious establishment, two sorts	44	179
,, ,, —See Charitable Institution.		
,, foundation, repair by stranger allowed	45	182
Place of worship—See Mesjid.		
Poor are beneficiaries when vaqf is vacant	15	80
"Poor" construction	93	371
Poor entitled to free habitation cannot be charged rent	98	400
Power of exchange of vaqf property is valid	18	90
,, of sale in mortgage	68	261
,, to sell and distribute price as alms, invalid	18	90
Pre-emption co-owner house over Ijaretein Vaqfs by Sacred Law	64	241
,, houses and dwellings, in respect of	64	241
,, no right in respect of Mulk on Muqata'a site	74	284
Preference of proofs	116	470
,, vaqf has none over other creditors of deceased	89	354
Prescription—actions relating to original dedication	106, 107	435
,, common establishments, none	111	449
,, ignorance of title, no excuse	110	444
,, in Cyprus— immoveable property	111	449 N.B.
,, interest and income	111	446
,, lunar year	111	448
,, may be pleaded with other defences	109	441
,, Mutevelli suing possessor as lessee	109	442
,, possession by ancestor and heir	109	440
,, ,, by grantor and grantee	108	439
,, ,, of Takhsisat land	111	447
,, ,, of vaqf property	108	437
,, property dedicated in favour of children from generation to generation	107	436
,, reversion of Takhsisat land	111	447
,, runs to time of action brought	109	443
,, vaqf money	108	438
Price on alienation, inheritance of	59	224
,, ,, recovery of	59	223
,, return of, on ouster	59, 60	225
Probability without proof not regarded	30	136
Proof not probability required	30	136
,, of claims by Mutevelli	86	339
,, of descent	103, 104	422, 423
,, of expenditure by Mutevelli	86	339
,, that ownership lapsed before dedications is required	30	136
Property held in Ijaretein cannot be dedicated	10, 11	63
,, not belonging to dedicator cannot be made vaqf, unless the owner subsequently consents	10, 11	63
,, not belonging to dedicator is not made vaqf, even if dedicator subsequently acquires it	10, 11	63
,, occupied may be made vaqf	10	62
,, of insolvent deceased, when it may be made vaqf	10	61
,, special exception of part from dedication	19	97
,, under lease, effect of dedication	9, 10	60
,, ,, ,, may be made vaqf	10	61
,, undivided share may be made vaqf, except for Mesjid or cemetery	11	64
,, wrongfully appropriated cannot be made vaqf	10, 11	63
Public Establishment, Ijaretein Vaqf turned into, should be made Muqata'a	74	286

	PAGE	ARTICLE
Purchase by Mutevelli out of income of vaqf	7, 8	55
,, ,, ,, dedicated money	8	55
Qaimaqam-i-Mutevelli, appointment of	78, 79	303
,, ,, appointed by Court to carry out alienation	54	206
,, ,, during absence of Mutevelli	78, 79	303
,, ,, for a lawsuit	78, 79	303
,, ,, meaning of	2	10
,, ,, to assent to transfer by or to Mutevelli	78, 79	303
,, ,, to lend vaqf money to Mutevelli	78, 79	303
,, ,, to take proceedings against Mutevelli	78, 79	303
,, ,, what Judge may appoint	79	305
,, ,, when Judge may appoint	78, 79	303
,, ,, where Mutevelli incapable	79	304
Qaim-i-Vaqf, meaning of	2	9
Qualification of grant by collateral document	104, 105	425, 428
Qowvvam, plural of Qaim	2	9
Recovery by stranger of a share of property made vaqf	11	64
,, of price on alienation	59	223
Redemption, stipulation against, invalid	66	250
Rey' Vaqf, meaning of	1	5
Refusal of dedication—See Dedication, refusal.		
Re-investment, leave of Judge to be obtained for	13	70
Re-instalment of depraved Mutevelli	82	325
Rejection by beneficiary at time of dedication	42	174
Release a bar	106	434
,, of debt by Mutevelli	85	336
Religion of dedicator and beneficiary need not be the same	8	57
,, difference of, when a bar to inheritance	50	193
Renewal of lease of Ijare-i-Vahide Vaqf, lessee has no right to	71	273
Repairs, a sum to be set aside from income for	92	366
,, by guardian for person under disability	56, 57	217
,, by lessee of vaqf property	97	396
,, contribution for, when given	64	242
,, loans and advances for	88	346
,, of house dedicated to be occupied	101	412
,, of house of which income is dedicated	101	413
,, of pious establishments by stranger	45	182
,, take precedence of grants	101	411
Rescission of alienation, option for	58, 59	220, 221, 222
,, of partition for excessive damage	61, 62	233
Reshid, meaning of	2	13
Resignation of Mutevelli	82	324
Return of price, on ouster	59, 60	225
Revocation of agent's authority	67	259
,, ,, dedication before decision of Judge	25	116
,, ,, ,, by will	27	122
,, ,, ,, ,, how made	27	122
,, ,, will by dedication	17	87
Rights attached to property pass on dedication of property	18	95
Sahiha Vaqf, Arazi Mirié acquired as Mulk and dedicated, is Sahiha	28	127
,, Vaqfs, Arazi Kharajié made vaqf are	28	125
,, ,, Arazi Ushrie made vaqf are	28	125
,, ,, can co-exist with Takhsisat	31	138
,, ,, meaning of	28	124
,, ,, Mevat land acquired as Mulk and dedicated, is Sahiha	28	126
Salaries, loans and advances not allowed for	88	349

	PAGE	ARTICLE
Salary and victuals given from vaqf are called Vazife	3	21
Sale—*See* Alienation.		
Sale, power of, in mortgage	68	261
Sened not necessary to complete sale of Ijareteinlu	53	200
Share undivided, alienation of	63, 64	240
Sick person, alienation by	54, 55	209,213
Simultaneous death of relations	49, 50	192
Slave cannot dedicate without permission of master	8	53(2)
Slavery a bar to inheritance	52	196
Sound mind, alienor must be of	53, 54	203
Stipulation against power of redemption, invalid	66	250
,, that building by Ijaretein tenant should belong to vaqf, of no force	70	268
Stranger, recovery by, of share of vaqf property	11	64
,, repair of pious establishment by	45	182
Succeeding Mutevelli can sue for loan	89	353
Ta'amul, meaning of	3	27
Takhsis are of two kinds	31	138
,, means the making of a Takhsisat Vaqf	31	138
,, true, irrevocable	31	138
,, untrue, revocable at will of Sultan	31	138
Takhsisat, meaning of	29	131
,, dedications, alterations	39	165
,, tithe of Ushrie land dedicated by the Sultan for charity supported by Beit-ul-mal, is	29	134
,, Vaqf, Arazi Mirié dedicated by Sultan without the ownership, is	28	127
,, ,, Kharaj of Kharajié lands dedicated by Sultan for charity supported by Beit-ul-mal, is	29	134
,, ,, may co-exist with Sahiha	31	139
,, Vaqfs, three kinds	30	137
,, ,, rights of owners of different kinds	30	137
,, ,, to what sort Land Law applies	30	137
Tax still payable after Kharajié land is dedicated	31	139
Teberru', meaning of	3	26
Teberru'at, plural of Teberru'	3	26
Temporary dedication, invalid	13	70
Tenant, Ijaretein, building by	70	268
,, ,, right of	45	188
,, ,, waste, liability for	69	263
,, Muqata'a, right to buildings, etc.	73	278
,, repairs by	97	396
,, —*See* Ijareteinlu, lessee.		
Tesjil-i-Istibdal, meaning of	4	32
,, Vaqf, meaning of	1	6
,, ,, necessary where property is bought from income of vaqf	7, 8	55
,, ,, not necessary when property bought with original vaqf	7, 8	55
Time—*See* Year.		
Tithe is payable after dedication of Ushrie land	31	139
Tithe still payable after Arazi Mirié granted as Mulk has been dedicated	31	139
Tree on Mulk site of dedicator cannot be dedicated alone	16, 17	85
Trees liable to be pulled down cannot be made vaqf	13	72
,, pass on dedication of site	18	95
,, —*See* Muqata'a Vaqf.		
Trespass—*See* Wrongful appropriation.		
,, by joint beneficiary	100	408
True and untrue vaqf may co-exist in the same subject	31	139
Uncertain condition, what is	12	67, 68
Undivided share, alienation of	63, 64	240
,, ,, may be dedicated	11	64

	PAGE	ARTICLE
Unowned share of Ijaretein Vaqf, grant of	63	239
Untrue and true vaqf may co-exist in the same subject	31	139
Useless charitable institution, income of, how spent	87	343
„ Mesjid, how dealt with	87	344
Ushrie Arazi Vaqf are Sahiha Vaqfs	28	125
„ land, tithe payable after dedication	31	139
Vacant Vaqfs, poor are beneficiaries	15	79
Vahide Vaqfs lessee has no right to renewal	71	273
„ „ letting at a Muqata'a rent	71	274
„ „ „ at Ijaretein rent	71, 72	275
„ „ of, rules for	71, 72	273, 275
„ „ term for which they may be left	70	271
„ „ what they are	70	270
Vaqfieh condition that building by tenant should belong to vaqf, invalid	70	268
„ differing from Defter Khaqani document	40	171
„ inconsistent terms in	42	173
„ is the judgment containing the terms of the vaqf	3	25
„ mistake in	41	172
Vaqif—See Dedicator.		
„ meaning of	1	1
Vaqf—See Dedication.		
Vaqfs discretionary	13	71
„ divided into revocable and irrevocable	1	4
„ has no preference over other creditor of deceased	89	354
„ hiring for, by Mutevelli	96	391
„ Irsadi, meaning of	1	3
„ land building by Mutevelli on	101	414
„ „ building on, by person other than Mutevelli	102	415
„ lands, different divisions of	43	178
„ „ divided into Sahiha and Takhsisat	28	124
„ letting of—See Letting of vaqfs.		
„ means a thing made vaqf	1	2
„ „ dedication	1	1
„ money of, expenditure on another	86	340
„ Mussaqafat and Mustaghelat alienation of, what is	3	17
„ offices—See Offices.		
„ property addition by beneficiary	100, 101	409, 410
„ „ destruction of	100	407
„ „ exchanged reverts into Mulk	26	119
„ „ exchange of, what may be taken in exchange	102	417
„ „ „ when allowed	102	416
„ „ „ irrevocable	103	420
„ „ recovered by third person reverts into Mulk	26	119
„ Sahiha—See Sahiha Vaqfs.		
„ „ and Takhsisat may co-exist in same land	31	139
„ Takhsisat—See Takhsisat.		
Vaqf Takhsisat, right of owners of different kinds	30	137
„ „ to what sort Land Law applies	30	137
„ „ three kinds	30	137
Vaqf vacant, poor are beneficiaries	15	79
„ what may be—an occupied property may be	10	62
„ „ „ Arazi Mirié by leave of the Sultan	29	132
„ „ „ Arazi Mirié dedicated by the Sultan	29	131
„ „ „ Arazi Mirié not acquired as Mulk without leave of Sultan, cannot	29	133
„ „ „ Arazi Mirié when acquired as Mulk, may be	28	127
„ „ „ as to trees planted on Arazi Mirié	13, 14	72
„ „ „ buildings liable to be pulled down, cannot	13, 14	72
„ „ „ buildings on Arazi Mirié as to	13, 14	72
„ „ „ building on land wrongfully appropriated, as to	13, 14	72
„ „ „ building on Mulk site	16, 17	85
„ „ „ „ on vaqf site	16, 17	85
„ „ „ „ „ „ as to	13, 14	72

			PAGE	ARTICLE
Vaqf what may be—defined property must be	11, 12	65
,, ,, ,, ghedik, cannot..	25	118
,, ,, ,, gift defective, as to	16	82
,, ,, ,, known property must be	11, 12	65
,, ,, ,, moveable property subject to immoveable property may be	9	59
,, ,, ,, moveable property where there is a custom	8, 9	58
,, ,, ,, must be immoveable property	8, 9	58
,, ,, ,, ,, Mal-i-Muteqavvim	6	46
,, ,, ,, mortgaged property may be	10	61
,, ,, ,, must be the property of dedicator at the time	10, 11	63
,, ,, ,, must be the thing itself	9, 10	60
,, ,, ,, not a debt, before payment except by bequest	9, 10	60
,, ,, ,, not necessary that property should be free from claim	9, 10	61
,, ,, ,, property held in Ijaretein, cannot ..	10, 11	63
,, ,, ,, property of insolvent deceased cannot, unless heirs first pay debts, or creditors consent	10, 11	63
,, ,, ,, property under lease may	9, 10	60
,, ,, ,, purchase by a defective sale, as to	16	82
,, ,, ,, purchase by an invalid sale, cannot ..	16	83
,, ,, ,, purchase not received, as to	16	81
,, ,, ,, ,, with an option to rescind	16	84
,, ,, ,, —See Property.		
,, ,, ,, the benefit of property without the property, cannot	9, 10	60
,, ,, ,, the thing must be capable of the consequences	7	50
,, ,, ,, thing sold with an option to rescind ..	16	84
,, ,, ,, trees liable to be pulled down, cannot ..	13, 14	72
,, ,, ,, trees on Mulk site of owners, cannot ..	16, 17	85
,, ,, ,, trees on vaqf site, as to	13, 14	72
,, ,, ,, undivided share, as to	11	64
,, ,, ,, vines on Mulk site of owner, cannot alone	16, 17	85
,, ,, ,, water as attached to water channels ..	18	91
,, ,, ,, water right to take, as attached to land ..	18	91
,, who may make—See Dedicator.		
Vazaif, plural of Vazife.		
Vazife, meaning of	3	21
Vines pass on dedication of site	18	95
,, on Mulk site of dedicator cannot be dedicated alone ..	16, 17	85
Vines—See Muqata'a Vaqf.		
Wages, increase of	91, 92	364
Waste, liability of Ijaretein tenant for	69	263
Water, dedication of	18	91
What may be made vaqf—See Vaqf, what may be made.		
Wife, dedication in favour of, until re-marriage	37	158
Will, dedication by	9,12,17,24	60,68,86,113
,, guardian under, may exercise power in his own favour ..	36	155
,, revocation, how made	27	122
,, revoked by subsequent dedication	17	87
Woman may be Mutevelli	75	289
Worship, place of—See Mesjid.		
Written grant cannot be varied by oral evidence ..	105	426
Wrongful appropriation damages	98	402
,, appropriator, who is	99	403
Wrongfully appropriated property cannot be made vaqf ..	10, 11	63
Year, how calculated	92	368
Zurriyet has same meaning as Nesl	3	24